1–3 JOHN

WESLEY BIBLE STUDIES

wphonline.com

Copyright © 2014 by Wesleyan Publishing House
Published by Wesleyan Publishing House
Indianapolis, Indiana 46250
Printed in the United States of America
ISBN: 978-0-89827-856-9
ISBN (e-book): 978-0-89827-857-6

CONTENTS

Introduction   5

1. Living in the Light
   1 John 1:1–7; 2:7–11   7

2. Victory Over Sin
   1 John 1:8 — 2:6, 12–14   16

3. Pursuing Truth
   1 John 2:18–29   25

4. Love Is Show and Tell
   1 John 2:15–17; 3:11–24   35

5. God Loves His Children
   1 John 3:1–10   44

6. True or False?
   1 John 4:1–6   53

7. The Source of All Love
   1 John 4:7–21   62

8. Three Spiritual Truths
   1 John 5:1–12   71

9. Praying with Confidence
   1 John 5:13–21   79

10. What a Journey!
    2 John 1–13   87

11. Imitate What Is Good
    3 John 1–14   96

Words from Wesley Works Cited   105

INTRODUCTION

Who's That Knocking at Your Door?

Knock! Knock! Is it a neighbor knocking at your door? He probably wants to borrow your lawn mower again. It might be a student selling magazine subscriptions to help fund her education. Or it might be a member of a cult wanting to divert your faith from the Bible.

Cults are active, aren't they? They regularly canvass neighborhoods, hoping to recruit new members. You have seen them. They are well dressed and carry an attaché case. If you show the slightest interest in their canned approach, they will reach into their case and pull out introductory literature. But if you plan to engage them in a discussion about their beliefs and yours, you had better be prepared. They are well versed in their dogma and are very deceptive!

Invariably, cults hold an erroneous view of Jesus' person and work. They reject the fact that He is both God and man and the fact that His shed blood was sufficient for the remission of sins. They also deny His bodily resurrection.

DÉJÀ VU!

Religious deception isn't a recent phenomenon. The aging apostle John exposed it in his letters and warned believers to remain in the truth. Cultic teaching about Jesus is at least two thousand years old. When John addressed his readers, he wanted them to resist Gnosticism, a heretical religious philosophy that boasted about its secret knowledge. The Gnostics believed all matter was evil, and therefore, Jesus could not have been God in the flesh. John called this denial the spirit of antichrist. The Gnostics also believed that what a person did in the body didn't matter because, after all, the body is inherently evil.

To combat Gnosticism and every heretical teaching about Jesus, John counseled believers how to walk in a manner that pleases God and honors Jesus as the Son of God, Savior, and Lord.

WALK THIS WAY!

We should walk as God's dear children. Because we are God's born ones, we should resemble Him in holiness and love. We should walk in the light, as Jesus is in the light. Unbelievers walk in darkness, but the lifestyle of believers should reflect the light that shone into our hearts through the gospel. The darkness of sin is behind us. Christ's Spirit empowers us to live in victory over sin. We should also walk in love—love for God and love for one another. As Jesus pointed out, love is the litmus test for declaring that we are His disciples (John 13:35). Further, we should walk in the truth. Allegiance to Jesus, who is the Truth, and allegiance to inspired truth, the Word of God, will protect us from the lies perpetrated by false teachers.

Finally, as we walk, we should stay in step with the Spirit. He desires to produce the fruit of holiness in our lives. A holy life offers a strong defense against false teaching and a positive testimony for the truth.

As you explore what the apostle John's letters teach about the walk that pleases God and refutes error, may you recognize that our risen Lord is walking with you!

LIVING IN THE LIGHT

1 John 1:1–7; 2:7–11

Jesus, the true Light, shows us how to live.

Gas lamps were a welcome phenomenon in the United States when they were introduced. In 1816 Baltimore was the first city in the United States to install public gas lighting, but by 1860 gas chandeliers, also called gaseliers, were popular, and before 1900 most major cities were lit by gas.

We have come far from those early days. Now lighting our homes is as easy as flipping a switch. Nevertheless, darkness envelops thousands of people around the world. It is spiritual darkness that only Jesus Christ can remove. He alone can transfer lives from darkness into His light. This study helps us appreciate the light, live in the light, and fellowship with one another in the light.

COMMENTARY

John was writing as an elder in the church at Ephesus. He was the pastor, bishop, mature believer, and one who was taught by Jesus himself. John was writing a general letter to believers everywhere with the particular people of his own church in mind. Much has been written of the author and the particular community for which he wrote, but we must understand community primarily in terms of a worshiping community, that is, a church.

Central to the church is the concept of fellowship. These verses address both divine/human fellowship (1:3) and interpersonal fellowship (2:9–10). These two aspects of fellowship come together in 1 John 1:7: "But if we walk in the light, as he is in the light, we have fellowship with one another, and the blood of Jesus, his Son, purifies us from all sin." We also find both types of fellowship in the Great Commandment: "'Love the Lord your God with all your heart and with all your soul and with all your strength and with all your mind'; and, 'Love your neighbor as yourself'" (Luke 10:27). Thus, to understand the church means we must understand Jesus, not as a man or a great teacher, but as the Christ, the Savior.

Therefore, the total context of these verses is Jesus and His church. In theological terms, the word for the study of the church is *ecclesiology*, and the word for studying Jesus as the Christ is *Christology*. In these verses, John expressed what theologians call a *christological ecclesiology*. It means that the church is defined by, in, and through Jesus as the Christ, the Savior. Thus, churchgoers are also defined the same way.

Most of the time we understand "if we walk in the light as he is in the light" to mean individual beliefs and actions—don't lie, cheat, steal, drink, smoke, or gamble. However, we rarely understand "walking in the light" in terms of our relationships. Yet 1 John 1:7 says, "But if we walk in the light, as he is in the light, *we have fellowship with one another*" (emphasis added), and that is clearly relational. Whatever our ethical and moral choices may be, their value is determined by how they preserve and protect our relationships with one another and with God. John asserted an intimate relationship between our actions, our fellowship with one another, and our salvation. In our actions, "we have fellowship with one another and the blood of Jesus, his Son, purifies us from all sin." Salvation, even though it deals with the individual, is a communal experience. *I* do not walk in the light so much as *we* walk in the light. The goal of Christian teaching is to affect a change in beliefs and behaviors. Such change is not simply in the individual for the sake of the individual, but in the individual for the sake of the community—the church.

Christology: How John Understood Jesus as the Christ (1 John 1:1–7)

John's primary understanding of Jesus as the Christ was as the one who **purifies us from all sin** (v. 7). Verse 7 is the climactic statement of verses 1–6. These building-block verses contain four primary characteristics of Jesus that reveal His ability to purify. According to John, Jesus is eternal, tangible, relational, and divine. Within the ancient world, these four characteristics were viewed as conceptual opposites. John's critics would charge that nothing could be both eternal and tangible, nor could anything be both relational and divine.

If something is tangible, it is physical and subject to decay, failure, and death. Similarly, if something is divine, it is self-sufficient, ruling out any true relational quality. For example, John 5:18 says, "For this reason the Jews tried all the harder to kill him; not only was he breaking the Sabbath, but he was even calling God his own Father, making himself equal with God." God's divinity required Him to be set apart from everything, to be God and God alone. This is why John was at pains to make the point that though the Word (eternal) became flesh (tangible) and dwelt among us (relational), He was "the glory of the One and Only" (divine), though He "came from the Father, full of grace and truth" (relational) (John 1:14).

John's knowledge of Jesus as the Christ centered on Jesus' ability to embody these seemingly opposite characteristics. Additionally, John's knowledge of salvation was believers' ability to embody these same characteristics **if we walk in the light, as he is in the light** (1 John 1:7). That is, as we are tangibly related to God the Father through Jesus the Son, we have an eternal status within the divine will. Again, in his gospel, John put it this way on the lips of Jesus: "For my Father's will is that everyone who looks to the Son and believes in him shall have eternal life, and I will raise him up at the last day" (John 6:40).

Eternal life is a divine relationship that exists through the bodily, tangible resurrection of Jesus and the promise of the same bodily, tangible resurrection of those who believe. The "last day" is the day when these seemingly opposite characteristics will be revealed to be not only harmonious but central characteristics of the life created by God, **which was from the beginning, which we have heard, which we have seen with our eyes, which we have looked at and our hands have touched**, and which **we proclaim concerning the Word of life** (1 John 1:1).

WORDS FROM WESLEY
1 John 1:5

God is light—The light of wisdom, love, holiness, glory. What light is to the natural eye, that God is to the spiritual eye: *And in him is no darkness at all*—No contrary principle. He is pure, unmixed light. (ENNT)

"And I heard a loud voice from the throne saying, 'Now the dwelling of God is with men, and he will live with them. They will be his people, and God himself will be with them and be their God. He will wipe every tear from their eyes. There will be no more death or mourning or crying or pain, for the old order of things has passed away'" (Rev. 21:3–4). This is the vision of the coexistence of the eternal and the tangible, of the relational and the divine. John understood this vision to be for "everyone who looks to the Son and believes in him" (John 6:40). Therefore, he wrote in our passage, **We proclaim to you what we have seen and heard, so that you also may have fellowship with us. And our fellowship is with the Father and with his Son, Jesus Christ. We write this to make our joy complete** (1 John 1:3–4). Note the similarity with Jesus' statement, "I have told you this so that my joy may be in you and that your joy may be complete" (John 15:11). John's knowledge of Christ was not for him only, and was in some ways incomplete unless he gave others the opportunity to share in it—thus, the church.

WORDS FROM WESLEY
1 John 1:7

But if we walk in the light—In all holiness, *as God is* (a deeper word than walk, and more worthy of God) *in the light*—Then we may truly say, *we have fellowship one with another*—We who have seen, and you who have not seen, do alike enjoy that fellowship with God: the imitation of God being the only sure proof of our having fellowship with Him. *And the blood of Jesus Christ his Son*—With the grace purchased thereby; *cleanseth us from all sin*—Both original and actual, taking away all the guilt and all the power. (ENNT)

Ecclesiology: How John Understood the Church (1 John 2:7–11)

John's concept of the church (his ecclesiology) was firmly built on his concept of Jesus as the Christ (his Christology). Consider the line of argument in Jesus' statements from John's gospel:

- "I am the light of the world. Whoever follows me will never walk in darkness, but will have the light of life" (8:12).
- "Put your trust in the light while you have it, so that you may become sons of light" (12:36).
- "If you love me, you will obey what I command" (14:15).
- "My command is this: Love each other as I have loved you. Greater love has no one than this, that he lay down his life for his friends" (15:12–13).

From this foundation, John wrote, **Dear friends, I am not writing you a new command but an old one, which you have**

had since the beginning. This old command is the message you have heard (1 John 2:7). In 3:11 of this letter, John stated explicitly, "This is the message you heard from the beginning: We should love one another." The question becomes, how could he follow 2:7 with the statement, **yet I am writing you a new command** (v. 8)?

WORDS FROM WESLEY
1 John 2:8

A commandment which, though it also was given long ago, yet is truly new in Him, and in you. It was exemplified in Him, and is now fulfilled by you in such a manner as it never was before. For there is no comparison between the state of the Old Testament believers, and that which ye now enjoy; the darkness of that dispensation is passed away; and Christ the true light now shineth in your hearts. (ENNT)

The answer is urgency. Because of John's Christology as examined above, John could say that the truth expressed in 15:12–13 of his gospel **is seen in him** (Jesus) **and you** (believers). Even more, **the darkness** (sin) **is** (currently) **passing and the true light is already shining** (1 John 2:8). While the command to love one another and have fellowship in the light of Christ is an old command, John was issuing it in a new sense of urgency in order to excite that urgency in the church. The old order of things was passing and a new order had begun. It is imperative that believers participate fully in the new order so that the way may be opened for whoever will believe to come in.

This letter is a practical summary of John's gospel: "I write these things to you who believe in the name of the Son of God so that you may know that you have eternal life" (1 John 5:13). According to John, the greatest threat to eternal life, and thus the church, is hate. **Anyone who claims to be in the light but hates** his brother is still in the darkness. Whoever loves his brother lives in the light, and there is nothing in him to make him stumble. But whoever hates his brother is in the darkness and walks around in the darkness; he does not know where he is going, because the darkness has blinded him (2:9–11).

WORDS FROM WESLEY

1 John 2:11

He that hateth his brother—And he must hate, if he does not love Him; there is no medium; *is in darkness*—In sin, perplexity, entanglement. He walketh in darkness, and knoweth not that he is in the high road to hell. (ENNT)

Hate destroys relationships. Hate destroys the tangible. "Do not be like Cain, who belonged to the evil one and murdered his brother" (3:12). Hate hides the eternal and the divine by clouding the one who hates in darkness. John began with the concept "God is light; in him there is no darkness at all" (1:5). Then he transferred the concept of light to the reality of love: "Whoever does not love does not know God, because God is love" (4:8). For the final step, in 4:16, John connected love directly with salvation: "And so we know and rely on the love God has for us. God is love. Whoever lives in love lives in God, and God in him."

John understood the church to be a community that loves the One it cannot see by loving the ones it can see. It is a community that accepts the reality it cannot see by rejecting the reality it can see. Why? Because the One whom it cannot see and the reality that it cannot see has been seen, and touched, and heard, in the person of Jesus of Nazareth, Son of Man and Son of God, the One who died and was raised again, the One who loved us more than life itself. John understood the church to be the continuing presence of Jesus on earth until He returns. Thus, there is no room for hate in the church, for the church is the light, the love, and the embodiment of God's salvation to a world lost in darkness. "If anyone obeys his word, God's love is truly made complete in him. This is how we know we are in him: Whoever claims to live in him must walk as Jesus did" (2:5–6). This is the true definition of a christological ecclesiology—a church that walks in the light as He is in the light.

DISCUSSION

Nobody would choose to live in perpetual darkness. Thankfully, Jesus delivered us from darkness, and now we live in the light—His light!

1. Compare John 1:1 and 1 John 1:1–2. Based on what John wrote in these passages, how would you describe Jesus Christ in your own words?

2. Do you believe genuine Christian fellowship can exist between a person who has been cleansed by Jesus' blood and a person who has not? Defend your answer.

3. Do you agree or disagree that it is possible to love an unbeliever without having fellowship with him or her?

4. What differences, if any, do you see between being in the light and walking in the light? Explain your answer.

5. How would you define Christian fellowship? Defend your definition.

6. If someone asked you to use a brief sentence to tell who Jesus is, what would your sentence be?

7. How might Christians relate to one another in ways that manifest their genuine love for Christ?

8. Do you think a constantly hateful person has genuinely trusted in Christ as Savior? Why or why not?

PRAYER

Father, help us to recognize when we walk in the darkness, draw close to You, and learn to live in Your light.

VICTORY OVER SIN

1 John 1:8—2:6, 12–14

All have sinned; all can be forgiven; all can choose to walk with God.

If you have your heart set on an antique confessional booth, you can find it in an antique store if you browse around long enough or search the Internet. But who needs to spend hard-earned money on a confessional booth, when we can confess our sins directly to God and receive immediate forgiveness and cleansing from our sin?

When a church planned to install a drive-up confessional, a church member asked sarcastically, "What will we call it, Toot 'n Tell?"

There is nothing flippant about confessing our sins. Sin is a serious offense against God, but as our study explains, forgiveness and victory over sin are available. We need to view our sin as God sees it and also acknowledge our deep need of His forgiveness.

COMMENTARY

Sin is a reality. However, it can be forgiven. Even more, it can be avoided. Today's passages do not lend themselves to defeatist attitudes, nor do they excuse the rationalization that "to err is human." True, humans do make mistakes, and not all mistakes are sin. It may be argued that a genuine mistake is never a sin, but that is an argument that masks the central point. Sin cannot be dismissed. It is real. It affects everyone.

Something is wrong in the world. There is violence, oppression, hatred, bigotry, and general unfairness. Some accept this as the way things are. For John, these things revealed something foundationally wrong. He immediately viewed this conceptual context in theological terms, namely sin.

But there is an answer, a remedy, an antidote, for sin— forgiveness from God through repentance and the blood of Jesus Christ. God does not forgive us because we are good. Instead, He sets us apart, making us holy. It is this God-given holiness that empowers us to change our emotions and behaviors away from sin.

John painted in black and white—no gray. "Dear children, do not let anyone lead you astray. He who does what is right is righteous, just as he is righteous. He who does what is sinful is of the devil, because the devil has been sinning from the beginning. The reason the Son of God appeared was to destroy the devil's work. No one who is born of God will continue to sin, because God's seed remains in him; he cannot go on sinning, because he has been born of God" (1 John 3:7–9). What is fascinating is that in our passages today, John wrote of sin in the past tense when speaking of believers. John was not writing to defeat those whose spirit is willing but whose flesh is weak. Instead, he wrote to remind believers of the strength given to the flesh through belief. These passages are a holiness manifesto designed to bolster us in the confidence we have in God's love to defeat sin. We have it, John declared, so let's live in it!

The Reality of Sin and Forgiveness (1 John 1:8–10)

Most people are uncomfortable with admitting that they sin. **If we claim to be without sin, we deceive ourselves and the truth is not in us. . . . If we claim we have not sinned, we make him out to be a liar and his word has no place in our lives** (vv. 8, 10). Ironically, in our society of addictions and dysfunction, it is a well-worn axiom that the first step to healing is to admit we have a problem. Here is the rub: We want the problem to be anything but sin. Sin denotes a responsibility that is all our own. We cannot share the responsibility for our sin with others. Whatever injustice we suffered as children or whatever debilitation has accompanied our existence, they differ significantly from our sin. Those other issues can be laid, at least partially, at the feet of others or at the doorstep of misfortune. Sin, however, is all our own, a willful turning from the good to the bad, an acceptance of and participation in evil for the sake of evil itself. To admit sin is to be naked before the world, uncovered from rationalizations and excuses. Admitting sin is to genuinely sing, "It's not my mother, not my father, not my sister, nor my brother, but it's me, O Lord, standing in the need of prayer."

Interestingly, though both verses 8 and 10 speak of sin, it is actually forgiveness that John is emphasizing. **If we confess our sins, he is faithful and just and will forgive us our sins and purify us from all unrighteousness** (v. 9). It was a common writing technique in biblical times to begin with one concept (sin in this case), introduce another concept (forgiveness), and return to the first concept (sin). It is called "bracketing," putting the most important issue in the middle to draw attention to it. This becomes obvious here with the following verse, which begins chapter 2, "My dear children, I write this to you so that you will not sin."

It seems the quickest path to sin is to deny its existence. Thus, it is true that the first and most important step to healing is to admit there is a problem. The problem with sin is that once we admit to it, we immediately realize we are enslaved to our sin and cannot free ourselves. As Paul lamented in Romans 7:14–21:

> We know that the law is spiritual; but I am unspiritual, sold as a slave to sin. I do not understand what I do. For what I want to do I do not do, but what I hate I do. And if I do what I do not want to do, I agree that the law is good. As it is, it is no longer I myself who do it, but it is sin living in me. I

know that nothing good lives in me, that is, in my sinful nature. For I have the desire to do what is good, but I cannot carry it out. For what I do is not the good I want to do; no, the evil I do not want to do—this I keep on doing. Now if I do what I do not want to do, it is no longer I who do it, but it is sin living in me that does it. So I find this law at work: When I want to do good, evil is right there with me.

What is the answer? "Who will rescue me from this body of death?" (Rom. 7:24). John answered in 1 John 1:9. And Paul, likewise, responded, "Thanks be to God—through Jesus Christ our Lord!" (Rom. 7:25). Just as we must acknowledge sin to be the problem, we must acknowledge Jesus to be the answer. We do not have the power to defeat sin. It is an internal, embedded impairment. The only remedy is to confess our general sinfulness, as well as specific sins, to God and accept that His forgiveness is effective in changing our fundamental understanding of and approach to our lives.

WORDS FROM WESLEY

1 John 1:9

Exactly agreeable to this are his words in the first chapter of this epistle (verse 5, &c.), "God is light, and in Him is no darkness at all. If we walk in the light—we have fellowship one with another, and the blood of Jesus Christ his Son cleanseth us from all sin." And again: "If we confess our sins, He is faithful and just to forgive us our sins, and to cleanse us from all unrighteousness." Now, it is evident, the apostle here also speaks of a deliverance wrought *in this world*. For he saith not, the blood of Christ will cleanse at the hour of death, or in the day of judgment, but, it "cleanseth," at the time present, "us," living Christians, "from all sin." And it is equally evident, that if *any sin* remain, we are not cleansed from *all sin:* If *any* unrighteousness remain in the soul, it is not cleansed from *all* unrighteousness. (WJW, vol. 6, 18)

Just as we have difficulty admitting to the reality of sin, we have more difficulty admitting to the reality of forgiveness. It is the reality of forgiveness that is both the cosmic focal point and the individual turning point of our lives according to John. That is the subject of the next passage.

WORDS FROM WESLEY
1 John 2:1

My beloved children—So the apostle frequently addresses the whole body of Christians. It is a term of tenderness and endearment, used by our Lord himself to His disciples (John 13:33). And perhaps many to whom St. John now wrote were converted by his ministry. It is a different word from that which is translated *little children* in several parts of the epistle, to distinguish it from which it is here rendered *beloved children. I write these things to you, that ye may not sin*—Thus he guards them beforehand against abusing the doctrine of reconciliation. All the words, institutions, and judgments of God are leveled against sin, either that it may not be committed, or that it may be abolished. *But if any one sin*—Let him not lie in sin, despairing of help; *we have an Advocate*—We have for our advocate not a mean person, but Him of whom it was said, This is my beloved Son: not a guilty person, who stands in need of pardon for himself; but *Jesus Christ the righteous*; not a mere petitioner, who relies purely upon liberality, but one that has merited, fully merited, whatever He asks. (ENNT)

Forgiveness as the Cosmic Focal Point of Life (1 John 2:1–2)

John placed individual sin within a cosmic scope. The picture of Jesus speaking to the Father on our behalf is a picture of the Father as the cosmic judge—not only our judge, but the judge of the whole world. For this reason, the salvation given by the Father through the Son is for the whole world. In an age where global travel was unknown, "the whole world" was a concept beyond imagination. For us today it would be "the whole universe." This is essential, since the effects of sin are beyond our imagination.

Thus the psalmist prayed, "Who can discern his errors? Forgive my hidden faults" (Ps. 19:12). It is only a cosmic God who searches all places who can "teach me wisdom in the inmost place . . . Create in me a pure heart . . . and renew a steadfast spirit within me" (Ps. 51:6, 10). For the individual to have certain hope, God must be the God of all.

WORDS FROM WESLEY

1 John 2:2

And he is the propitiation—The atoning sacrifice, by which the wrath of God is appeased; *for our sins*—Who believe: *and not for ours only, but also for the sins of the whole world*—Just as wide as sin extends, the propitiation extends also. (ENNT)

Forgiveness as the Turning Point of Individual Life (1 John 2:3–6)

God's forgiveness is effective in our lives because it not only removes sin, but replaces sin with love, divine love. Knowing God is not simply an intellectual exercise. We cannot know enough about God to bring about the substantive change in our lives that sin requires. The value of the intellectual knowledge of God is that the more we know of Him, the more we are convinced of our sin and our need for Him and His forgiveness. Paul observed, "Indeed I would not have known what sin was except through the law. For I would not have known what coveting really was if the law had not said, 'Do not covet'" (Rom. 7:7).

The insidious nature of sin is that sometimes the more we know about good and evil, the more evil we do. Paul continued in Romans 7:8 to say, "But sin, seizing the opportunity afforded by the commandment, produced in me every kind of covetous desire." That is, we begin to rationalize what it really means to sin, differentiating, for instance, between egregious lies and "little white lies." In this process, we are still relying on our own ability to discern what is right and to do what is right. We have placed our confidence in our willpower, and we have not resigned ourselves to God's love.

When **God's love is truly made complete in** us (1 John 2:5), we pray with the psalmist, "Search me, O God, and know my heart; test me and know my anxious thoughts. See if there is any offensive way in me, and lead me in the way everlasting" (Ps. 139:23–24). To **walk as Jesus did** (1 John 2:6) is to be able to say to the Father, "Not my will, but yours be done" (Luke 22:42; see also Matt. 26:39; Mark 14:36). This can only be accomplished if we "know" God as the One who has personally forgiven us, removed our sin, and replaced it with His love.

Forgiveness as the Power of Life (1 John 2:12–14)

This section is part of a poem or a song, maybe written by John, or maybe used by him because it was familiar and made his point.

I write to you, dear children,
because your sins have been forgiven on account of his name.
I write to you, fathers,
because you have known him who is from the beginning.
I write to you, young men,
because you have overcome the evil one.
I write to you, dear children,
because you have known the Father.
I write to you, fathers,
because you have known him who is from the beginning.
I write to you, young men,
because you are strong,
and the word of God lives in you,
and you have overcome the evil one.

Children who have received earthly life from an earthly father have received eternal life through the forgiveness of a heavenly Father. Fathers who have given earthly life and protection to their children have received life and protection from a heavenly Father. Young men whose charge it is to work and provide and to fight to preserve safety have been strengthened and protected on high from evil itself. Everything that was considered relationally essential to provide life, identity, and sustenance had been established in God from the beginning and removed from the influence of evil in the present through forgiveness.

Notice the verb tense used by John—you *have been forgiven* . . . you *have known* the Father . . . you *have overcome the evil one* (vv. 12–14, emphasis added). What we have is victory. Let's live in it! Who we have is God. Let's live in Him!

WORDS FROM WESLEY

1 John 2:12

Because, your sins are forgiven you—As if he had said, This is the sum of what I have now written. He then proceeds to other things, which are built upon this foundation. (ENNT)

DISCUSSION

Honesty prompts us to admit we are sinners, but grace prompts us to rejoice in forgiveness.

1. Why do you agree or disagree that 1 John 1:9 is *not* a promise for lost sinners?

2. Would you agree that a person who claims he or she does not sin is in denial? Explain.

3. Why don't we have the power in ourselves to deal with the sin problem?

4. When God forgives sin, what resources does He make available to the forgiven person?

5. Why do you agree or disagree that if we call something a necessary evil, it soon seems more and more necessary and less and less evil?

6. In 1 John 2:12–14, John addressed children, fathers, and young men. If you were given a brief opportunity to address these three groups in your church, what would you say to each of them?

PRAYER

Father, forgive us for our sins and help us to change our ways. Thank You for Your grace, mercy, love, and forgiveness.

PURSUING TRUTH

1 John 2:18–29

Followers of Christ must pursue truth and avoid error.

For centuries the subject of the Antichrist's identification has fascinated Christians. In the early centuries of Christianity, many identified him as the Roman emperor. In later centuries, Christians assumed this or that pope deserved the ignominious title. In recent times, many have pinned the tag on a powerful politician or a deceptive religious leader. Even Santa Claus has worn the label.

No one can assert positively that *the* Antichrist is alive today, but we can say for sure that the spirit of antichrist is alive and active. This study shows us how to identify the spirit of antichrist, and it motivates us to hold tightly to the truth that Jesus is the Son of God.

COMMENTARY

Just before Easter 2006, the front pages of many newspapers around the world contained stories about the uncovered fourth-century Gnostic manuscript *The Gospel of Judas*. One headline read, "New-found gospel makes Judas a hero" (*National Post*, Toronto, Apr. 7, 2006). Weeks later, the release of the film based on Dan Brown's 2003 best-seller, *The Da Vinci Code*, was likewise uncritically heralded by the world's presses for its understanding of Jesus. In both cases, fantastic claims were made about the recovery of some pristine Christianity and alternate truths. Together, these releases have forced Christians to think more deeply about what they believe and why their beliefs are more valid than others.

Alternate understandings of Jesus and the Christian faith are not new occurrences. They have been part of church life since the beginning and were felt even in the first century. In several New Testament passages, the biblical authors gave us hints of division, different thinking, error, and heresy. None perhaps more so than John, who, on several occasions in his short letter, addressed those who speak erroneously about Jesus. What makes this a matter of critical importance is that John implied that one's eternal destiny is linked to right thinking about Christ. John began his letter stressing the importance of walking in the light (1:7), obeying the commands of God (2:3, 17), and loving others (2:7), stating clearly that those who do the will of God live forever (2:17). In what follows, we learn that it is not just how one lives that is important. How one thinks and particularly what one thinks about Jesus is of equal importance when it comes to one's eternal destiny (2:24, 25; compare 5:11–13).

The Last Hour (1 John 2:18)

The phrase **the last hour** should be considered in light of related phrases such as "the last days" (Isa. 2:2; Hos. 3:5; Acts 2:17) and "the day of the Lord" (Isa. 13:6; Joel 2:1; 2 Thess. 2:2). The earliest believers lived with the expectation that the end was fast approaching when Christ would return and establish a new kingdom of righteousness (Matt. 24:34). The time between Christ's first and second advents was considered "the last days" (Acts 2:17). The idea of **the last hour** (1 John 2:18) was a note of urgency; the end was imminently near, indeed.

There are no easy answers as to why another nineteen hundred years have gone by since John declared that the end was near. Events in his world led him to suspect that time was short. There is a strain of New Testament thought that points to signs of the end and suggests that when they appear, one should get ready. This is apparent in Matthew 24, in which we are told to learn from the fig tree: "As soon as its twigs get tender and its leaves come out, you know that summer is near. Even so, when you see all these things, you know that it is near, right at the door" (vv. 32–33). John saw the arrival of "antichrists" as such a sign and issued a warning. Another strain of New Testament thought, however, states that we cannot know when Christ will return. Matthew wrote, "No one knows about that day or hour" (24:36; see also 24:42, 44, 45–51; 25:1–13). This strain of thought suggests that believers should be ready at all times for the return of Christ. The duty of believers is now to be ready, to live as if every hour were **the last hour** (1 John 2:18).

WORDS FROM WESLEY

1 John 2:18

Little children, it is the last time—The last dispensation of grace, that which it to continue to the end of time, is begun; *ye have heard that antichrist cometh*—Under the term antichrist, or the spirit of antichrist, he includes all false teachers, and enemies to the truth, yea, whatever doctrines or men are contrary to Christ. It seems to have been long after this, that the name of *antichrist* was appropriated to that grand adversary of Christ, the man of sin (2 Thess. 2:3). Antichrist, in St. John's sense, that is, antichristianism, has been spreading from his time till now; and will do so, till that great adversary arises, and it destroyed by Christ's coming. (ENNT)

Many Antichrists Have Come (1 John 2:18–19)

In 4:3, John indicated that "the spirit of the antichrist" had been prophesied. He may have been thinking of Jesus' words, "Many will come in my name, claiming, 'I am he!' and will deceive many" (Mark 13:6; see also 13:21; Matt. 24:5, 24). This saying is not an exact fit, however, because it indicates that the "deceivers" would claim to be the returned Christ. In contrast, John's "antichrists" would merely teach falsehood about Jesus.

The term *antichrist* occurs in the New Testament only in John's letters (2:18, 22; 4:3; 2 John 7). A thorough study of the word may include thinking about like concepts: the "man of lawlessness" (2 Thess. 2:1–12), "the abomination that causes desolation" (Mark 13:14; Dan. 11:31; 12:11), and the idea of the beast and false prophet (Rev. 13:19; 16:13; 19:20; 20:10). We can, nonetheless, learn a great deal about the antichrist(s) from John's letters themselves. John referred not to just one antichrist, but to **many antichrists** (1 John 2:18). These had actually been members of the church at one time but had lapsed. **They went out from us, but they did not really belong to us** (v. 19). John considered them to have been imbued with the spirit of the antichrist (4:3) such that the very power of the antichrist was speaking error through them. He called them liars (2:22), "false prophets" (4:1), and deceivers (2:26; 2 John 7) because of what they taught about Jesus.

The false teachings of the antichrists may be outlined in the chart below.

FALSE TEACHING OF THE ANTICHRISTS	ASSOCIATED SCRIPTURE
Denial of Jesus' messianic status	"Who is the liar? It is the man who denies that Jesus is the Christ" (1 John 2:22; compare 5:1).
Denial of the relationship between the Father and the Son	"Such a man is the antichrist— he denies the Father and the Son" (1 John 2:22). Note additionally 2:23–25; 4:15; 5:9–12. *continued*

FALSE TEACHING OF THE ANTICHRISTS	ASSOCIATED SCRIPTURE
Denial that Jesus had come in the flesh	"This is how you can recognize the Spirit of God: Every spirit that acknowledges that Jesus Christ has come in the flesh is from God, but every spirit that does not acknowledge Jesus is not from God. This is the spirit of the antichrist, which you have heard is coming and even now is already in the world" (1 John 4:2–3). "Many deceivers, who do not confess Jesus as coming in the flesh, have gone out into the world. Any such person is the deceiver and the antichrist" (2 John 7).

It is unclear to whom we should attribute these errors. Some scholars have tried to see Jewish opposition within the church denying Jesus' messianic status. Others have posited a link with an early form of Gnosticism. Gnosticism took many forms and flourished in the second through fourth centuries. One of its key doctrines was that God was spirit and so holy and pure that He would never contaminate himself with what was material, earthly, and polluted. It was impossible, therefore, in Gnostic thinking, for God to become incarnate in any real sense. Some Gnostics, therefore, saw Christ as a spirit or phantom who only appeared to be a physical presence and only appeared to suffer on the cross. Against this John wrote of having "seen," "heard," and "touched" the Lord (1:1–4). John perceived that he was in a battle for truth and for the hearts and souls of his flock. It was a battle not unlike that faced today by believers who are encountering a tremendous proliferation of philosophies and wisdoms.

In the midst of the pluralism of the age and the different views of Christ being touted as correct, it is sometimes difficult to know where truth lies. As an eyewitness of Jesus (1 John 1:1–4; 4:14), John provided reassurance for his flock. The apostle above all had authority to teach about Jesus and His personhood. Regardless of how much the deceivers' wisdom might tickle the ears of those who heard them, John had one great edge: He had been there. He had seen, heard, and touched the Lord. He above all could say, "Jesus is the Messiah, God with us."

Anointing from the Holy One (1 John 2:20, 27)

John contrasted those who "went out from us" (v. 19) with his readers who had **an anointing from the Holy One** (v. 20) and had knowledge. In the Old Testament, anointing was the privilege of key individuals, such as those who would be priests, kings, or prophets. After Pentecost, anointing is now the privilege of all who believe (see the prophecies in Jer. 31:31–34; Joel 2:28). Some interpreters link anointing by the Holy One with the coming of God's Spirit (2:20; 3:24; 4:2; 4:13). Others, drawing on thoughts in 2:24 and 27, suggest that the anointing is to be connected with the word of truth that believers had heard in the beginning. Perhaps we should not try to separate these two concepts since in Acts, baptism of the Spirit is related to encountering the Word. Note how the two come together in the words, "the Holy Spirit came on all who heard the message" (Acts 10:44).

WORDS FROM WESLEY

1 John 2:20

But ye have an anointing—A chrism; perhaps so termed in opposition to the name of antichrist, an inward teaching from the Holy Spirit, whereby *ye know all things*—Necessary for your preservation from these seducers, and for your eternal salvation. (ENNT)

All of You Know the Truth (1 John 2:20–26)

The wording again hints that John's opponents taught something akin to Gnostic thought. Another element of Gnosticism was the claim to have secret knowledge related to God, Jesus, and the way to heaven. Knowledge was all important to Gnostics and, interestingly, the Greek word *gnosis* that is used in this verse—from which the word *Gnostic* derives—actually means knowledge or esoteric knowledge. In 2:18–29, John appears to have been "taking a shot" at his opponents, saying, "The antichrists may claim knowledge, but you really know." **The truth** (v. 20) is the word they (the readers) had heard **from the beginning** (v. 24), and if they remained in the truth about Jesus, who is the Messiah (v. 22), the true Son of the Father in heaven (vv. 22–24), and who has come in the flesh (4:2), they would gain God's promise of **eternal life** (2:25). Jesus, properly understood, is the way to heaven. As John would state clearly later, "And this is the testimony: God has given us eternal life, and this life is in his Son. He who has the Son has life; he who does not have the Son of God does not have life" (5:11–12; compare John 14:6). It should be noted that the context in 1 John 2:18 suggests that "having the Son" involves right thinking about who Jesus is and what God did through Him. Again, the best source of truth about Jesus comes in the testimony of the eyewitnesses who had seen, heard, and touched Him. The word of the gospel preached by John, confirmed by the Holy Spirit, had anointed the readers in truth so they may have confidence at the time Jesus comes again and enter into His blessed presence for an eternity (2:28).

You Do Not Need Anyone to Teach You (1 John 2:27–29)

Because of what was initially taught, John's flock had no further need of teaching. This ought not be taken to mean that believers have no more to learn. As with all persons, Christians can never get enough wisdom. John, however, was thinking specifically of the erroneous teaching of the antichrists about Jesus. Believers, he implied, have no need of further teaching about Christ other than that handed on to them by the apostles and ministers of the Word.

WORDS FROM WESLEY

1 John 2:27

Ye need not that any should teach you, save as that anointing teacheth you—Which is always the same, always consistent with itself. But this does not exclude our need of being taught by them who partake of the same anointing: *of all things*—Which it is necessary for you to know: *and is no lie*—Like that which antichrist teaches. (ENNT)

Often in the church, salvation is portrayed as being the result of faith and the behavior that derives from faith. John made it clear here that it is not just any faith that leads to salvation, but true faith, true belief, right thinking about Jesus and all God accomplished in Him. Christian preaching does not always remind us that theology is important too. We must stick to the teaching that was handed down from the beginning by the "eyewitnesses and servants of the word" (see Luke 1:2). In this day and age in which false teaching and alternate views of Jesus receive so much press—such as was the case with *The Da Vinci Code* and the publication of *The Gospel of Judas*—it is even more important for Christians to know the truth that was passed on to us by those who were actually there. God was indeed in Jesus and dwelt among us.

WORDS FROM WESLEY

1 John 2:29

Every one—And none else, *who practiseth righteousness*—From a believing loving heart, *is born of him*—For all His children are like himself. (ENNT)

DISCUSSION

Believers should recognize the truth because they personally know Jesus, who is the truth. They can distinguish the Word of Christ from the false words of antichrists.

1. Read 1 John 2:18. Why do you agree or disagree that we are living in the last moments of the last hour?

2. What is your opinion of setting a date for Jesus' return? Explain your answer.

3. What might we do or not do if we lived as if every hour were "the last hour"?

4. Compare 1 John 2:18, 22; 4:3; and 2 John 7 with Revelation 13:11–17. Do you think the activities described in the Revelation passage reflect the spirit of antichrist? Why or why not?

5. Why is the incarnation of Christ essential to our faith?

6. How would you answer someone who claimed Jesus was just a god?

7. How do you assess the level of sound Bible teaching in today's preaching and in Christian books? Defend your answer.

PRAYER

Father, please give us a correct understanding of who Jesus is, that we might recognize truth from falsehood and be peacefully confident of Your Son's return.

LOVE IS SHOW AND TELL

1 John 2:15–17; 3:11–24

True Christian belief is demonstrated by genuine love.

One way to trap a monkey is to fill a hollow, narrow-necked gourd with nuts and set it where a monkey can see it. The monkey will reach into the gourd and grab a handful of nuts. But then its hand will be too wide to extract from the gourd, and will find itself trapped by its greed.

This study explains that we must not reach for what the evil world system offers. Instead, we should do God's will, and love Him and our fellow Christians. Love for the evil world system leads to a worthless end, but doing the will of God leads to great gain. So when the Devil sets the trap for us, let's not let him make monkeys of us.

COMMENTARY

The criteria for identifying true Christian belief and practice was explained by John in three statements that form the basic outline of this letter: (1) True Christian belief is connected with righteous living. False teaching and teachers are false first of all because they live false lives. They do not ethically live up to the standard of their own teaching. (2) True Christian belief is connected with a genuine love for fellow Christians. False teaching and teachers are divisive and fall into haughty exclusivism. (3) True Christian belief is connected with the belief in Jesus as the incarnate Christ. The false teachers of John's day denied that God had revealed himself in human flesh. These three criteria became John's test for orthodoxy: righteousness, love for other believers, and correct Christology.

A couple of the words John used in this study passage are interesting. The first is the word *world*. This word is found in four books written by the apostle. The word *world* appears seventy-eight times in John's gospel. It occurs twenty-two times in 1 John. It is found once in 2 John and six times in Revelation. This totals 107 occurrences of *world* in John's writings. The word has three connotations: (1) the cosmos created by God, as in John 1:10; (2) individuals who inhabit the created world, as in John 3:16; and (3) an alternate world system, with its own values, energized by Satan and opposed to God, as in John 15:18–19. It is important to understand John's use of *world* in this epistle. Also, the term *dear children* is used eight times in this first epistle (2:1, 12, 18, 28; 3:7, 18; 4:4; 5:21). This term implies a limited circle of Christians with whom John was closely acquainted.

Do Not Love the World (1 John 2:15–17)

One of the three criteria for true Christian belief is the correct expression of love. That is the theme of this text. The manner in which it is written is interesting. When a command is stated in the negative, it becomes a prohibition. This is what we have here. The prohibition **do not love the world** (v. 15) prohibits a continuous action or a lifestyle of loving the wrong object. As noted above, *world* has three meanings. This prohibition cannot be against loving God's created world; just the opposite should be the case. Christians should lead the way in the proper care of God's universe. This is not just for the sake of the environment, but also because this is our Father's world. Neither is the prohibition against loving the inhabitants of this world. That leaves the third option, and the prohibition is against a lifestyle that loves a world system that is against God and is committed to evil. Why? Because an individual cannot love, in the strong sense of this word, two opposing entities. As Jesus himself stated, "No one can serve two masters" (Matt. 6:24). **If anyone loves the world, the love of the Father is not in him** (1 John 2:15). The phrase **love of the Father** can be understood in two ways. First, it could mean that the love *from* the Father is not in the person. But God's love is not conditioned on our being lovable and loving ourselves. God loves the individual even when that love is not returned. The second possible meaning is that the love *for* the Father is not in the person. This must be what John intended here. One cannot have both love for the world and love for God at the same time.

WORDS FROM WESLEY

1 John 2:16

The desire of the flesh—Of the pleasure of the outward senses, whether of the taste, smell, or touch: *the desire of the eye*—Of the pleasures of imagination (to which the eye, chiefly, is subservient); of that internal sense, whereby we relish whatever is grand, new, or beautiful: *the pride of life*—All that pomp in clothes, houses, furniture, equipage, manner of living, which generally procure honour from the bulk of mankind, and so gratify pride and vanity. It therefore directly includes the desire of praise, and remotely, covetousness. All these desires are not from God, but from the prince of this world. (ENNT)

It may at times be difficult to determine exactly the object of an individual's love. How does it become evident whether one has love for God or the world? John mentioned three traits that indicate a love for the world. First, John mentioned **the cravings of sinful man** (v. 16). The word *craving* indicates unregulated, fleshly desires. The second trait is **lust of his eyes**, where the word **lust** indicates strong desire or passion. The third trait is **the boasting of what he has and does** that points to pride and boasting arrogance. Together, these three traits not only characterize a love for the world, but they reflect the corruption of a world system. **Everything in the world** (v. 16) either promotes or is qualified by the **cravings of sinful man, the lust** of the eye, or **boasting**.

Consider these three traits in regard to the temptation of Jesus Christ in the wilderness (Luke 4:1–13). The temptation to turn stones to bread was a temptation to satisfy physical cravings. The temptation to look at and potentially own the kingdoms of the world was the temptation to satisfy the lust of the eyes. The temptation for Jesus to throw himself down from the highest point of the temple was a temptation to satisfy boasting of what one has and does. All three come from this world system of corrupt values and thinking.

The source of the three traits is clear—**not from the Father but from the world** (1 John 2:16). **Do not love the world** (v. 15) because it produces characteristics such as the three listed here. But that is not the only reason not to love the world. The world is temporary. John reminded us that **the world and its desires pass away** (v. 17). The verb is present tense and indicates the world is in the process of passing away even as John wrote this letter. In contrast, **the man who does** (is doing) **the will of God** (now) **lives forever** (v. 17).

WORDS FROM WESLEY

1 John 2:17

The world passeth away, and the desire thereof—That is, all that can gratify these desires passeth away with it: *but he that doth the will of God*—That loves God, not the world, *abideth*—In the enjoyment of what He loves, *for ever*. (ENNT)

We Should Love One Another (1 John 3:11–15)

With this paragraph, we are introduced to the positive statement on love. **We should love one another** (v. 11) is the exhortation to a continual, habitual attitude of love. This commandment is not new, however. **You heard** it **from the beginning** (v. 11), and so John used an Old Testament example to illustrate the issue of love in action. The example centers on a brother by the name of Cain. John warned his readers, **do not be like Cain** (v. 12) because he was a murderer, but also because of who controlled him: **Cain . . . belonged to the evil one** (v. 12). The word **murder** used in this text is usually associated with the slaying of animals. It means to slaughter, kill, or butcher. It is used here of a violent killing. This violent killing was brought about because Cain hated Abel because his actions were righteous and Cain's were evil.

But why were Cain's actions evil and his brother's righteous? The story is told in Genesis 4. One suggestion as to why Cain's actions were evil is that he brought the wrong kind of offering to the Lord. He brought some of the fruits of the soil. Abel, his brother, brought fat portions from some of the firstborn of his flock. Later revelation regarding the laws and instructions for sacrifice offerings (Lev. 1:1—7:38) would make a clear distinction between a blood offering and a non-blood offering. It is possible that God gave these two brothers private instructions on proper offerings and Cain did not heed this instruction. This would account for the fact that God did not look with favor on his offering. Another possible reason why Cain's offering was not accepted deals with the element of faith. The New Testament states, "By faith Abel offered God a better sacrifice" (Heb. 11:4). This suggests it was not necessarily the kind of offering but Abel's faith that accompanied his offering that God took note of and acknowledged.

Now to the bigger picture. **Do not be surprised . . . if the world hates you** (1 John 3:13). The two Old Testament brothers represent the struggle between two competing worldviews. The two lifestyles of righteousness and evil are in a constant struggle. Do not be surprised. It is a struggle of life and death. This is how we use these terms in normal conversation. However, in spiritual matters, it is just the opposite. We are by natural birth, spiritually dead. God's grace, however, enables us to pass **from death to life** (v. 14). The proof that we have **passed from death to life** is that **we love our brothers** (v. 14).

We Know What Love Is (1 John 3:16–20)

To help us begin to understand the apostle's emphasis on love, he reminded his readers of the prime example of love—the passion of Jesus Christ. **Jesus Christ laid down his life for us** (v. 16). This phrase captures the vicarious, substitutionary death of our Lord. He gave himself for our sins (Gal. 1:4). This is the prime example of love. And because of this example, **we ought to lay down our lives for our brothers** (1 John 3:16). The Christian is morally obligated to respond to needs in the same manner as Jesus did (2:6). John used a hypothetical situation to illustrate the point. **If anyone has material possessions** (things pertaining to life, possessions, wealth) **and sees** (observes, notices, watches) **his brother in need** (3:17), he must respond appropriately. There is more than just a casual glance implied in John's situation. To observe such a lack should produce a response of wanting to help the fellow Christian. But what if he **has no pity on him** (v. 17)? No pity will mean no response. Jesus did not respond that way (Matt. 25:34–40). But if the believer's heart is unmoved, **how can the love of God be in him** (1 John 3:17)? The answer is obvious. If God's love is in a person, the same love will become the source of loving action in the believer's community.

Dear children, let us not love with words . . . but with actions (v. 18). The Christian response of love is not merely outward (with words or tongue), but of the total person. A lack of proper Christian response should bother us. **Whenever our hearts condemn us** (v. 20) is used here in the sense of conscience. But if our hearts condemn us, **God is greater than our hearts, and he knows everything** (v. 20). On the other hand, if our hearts do not condemn us, this serves as proof that **we belong to the truth** (v. 19) because we draw power from the truth that dwells within, and that power enables us to respond in a loving manner.

WORDS FROM WESLEY
1 John 3:17

But whoso hath this world's good—Worldly substance, far less valuable than life, *and seeth his brother have need*—(The very sight of want knocks at the door of the spectator's heart) *and shutteth up*—Whether asked or not, *his bowels of compassion from him, how dwelleth the love of God in him?*—Certainly not at all, however he may talk (ver. 18), of loving God. (ENNT)

Confidence before God (1 John 3:21–24)

In one sense of the word, a loving response to our brother or sister in need brings its own reward. But God's grace is greater than that. A clear conscience means **we have confidence before God** (v. 21). The word **confidence** is found four times in 1 John (2:28; 3:21; 4:17; 5:14), and in each case it denotes the confidence believers enjoy before God. They have this confidence because they "continue in him" (2:28), because their **hearts do not condemn** them (3:21), and because "love is made complete among" them (4:17). This leads to confidence in prayer (3:21; 5:14). This leads to another blessing in that we **receive from him anything we ask** (3:22; Matt. 7:7–8). But isn't **anything** too vague or doesn't it promise too much? On the contrary, a Christian open to God will **obey his commands and do what pleases him** (1 John 3:22). Such a person will not ask unwisely, not from a fleshly spirit. John summarized the commands by mentioning one command: **to believe in the name . . . and to love one another** (v. 23). Christians who believe and love **live in him, and he in them** (v. 24). If someone would ask **how we know that he lives in us** (v. 24), the answer is simply that our knowledge is based on the Holy Spirit bearing witness to our spirits that this is in fact a true relationship. The witness of the Spirit becomes the ultimate proof.

WORDS FROM WESLEY

1 John 3:24

This is that love on which the apostle John so frequently and strongly insists: "This," saith he, "is the message that ye heard from the beginning, that we should love one another" (1 John 3:11). . . .

All men approve of this; but do all men practice it? Daily experience shows the contrary. Where are even the Christians who "love one another as He hath given us commandment?" How many hinderances lie in the way! The two grand, general hinderances are, First, that they cannot all think alike; and, in consequence of this, Secondly, they cannot all walk alike; but in several smaller points their practice must differ in proportion to the difference of their sentiments.

But although a difference in opinions or modes of worship may prevent an entire external union; yet need it prevent our union in affection? Though we cannot think alike, may we not love alike? May we not be of one heart, though we are not of one opinion? Without all doubt, we may. Herein all the children of God may unite, notwithstanding these smaller differences. These remaining as they are, they may forward one another in love and in good works. (WJW, vol. 5, 493)

DISCUSSION

The Holy Spirit has shed God's love into our hearts, but how we direct and display this love are matters of great importance.

1. Can a Christian care for the environment without violating the command, "Do not love the world"? Why or why not?

2. How does the Devil tempt us through the cravings of the flesh, the lust of the eyes, and the boasting of what we have or have done?

3. Read Luke 4:1–13. What resource did Jesus use to overthrow the Devil's temptations? How might we use this resource successfully when he tempts us?

4. What motivation do you find in 1 John 3:17 for living for God instead of for worldly purposes?

5. What do you learn from the bad example Cain set?

6. Why do you agree or disagree that Christians are becoming a despised minority?

7. What do you learn about genuine love from Jesus' example? How can you apply what you learn?

PRAYER

Father, give us opportunities today to love others in action and in truth. Help us faithfully obey You that we may stand confidently before You.

GOD LOVES HIS CHILDREN

1 John 3:1–10

God loves His children and proves it.

According to *Science Daily* (June 12, 2012), "a father's love contributes as much—and sometimes more—to a child's development as does a mother's love." The report is based on an analysis of research about the power of parental rejection and acceptance in shaping our personalities as children and into adulthood.

Ronald Rohner of University of Connecticut and coauthor of the study concludes that "fatherly love is critical to a person's development. The importance of a father's love should help motivate many men to become more involved in nurturing child care."

As our study of 1 John 3:1–10 reveals, our heavenly Father's love influences us to develop into the kind of children He wants us to be.

COMMENTARY

First John 3:1–10 is a powerful passage showing the complete and utter incompatibility between Christians and sin. At the time of this letter's writing, heretics (John called them "antichrists" in 1 John 2) were seeking to lead believers astray with what would later be known as Gnosticism. John gave us hints in this letter of what they believed every time he used the phrase "if we claim" or "anyone who claims" (see 1:6, 8, 10; 2:6, 9). These early Gnostics, in addition to denying the fundamental truth of who Jesus is, believed sin was inconsequential. They thought they were saved and perfected by their secret knowledge (*gnosis*), and what they did in the body had no effect on their spirit (and so it couldn't properly be called "sin" at all). These antichrists were claiming their secret knowledge proved that they were the true children of God and that the Christians in John's audience were deficient in their knowledge and experience. How were the early Christians to know what was true? How could they be sure of their own salvation?

John set out in this letter to give his readers tests by which to discern truth and error. And one of those tests has to do with sin. Jesus had warned John and the other disciples that false prophets would come one day, but they would be readily recognizable by their fruit (Matt. 7:15–21). The early Gnostics made great claims, but their lives of sin betrayed their true nature.

Children of God Live in the Promise of the Second Coming (1 John 3:1–3)

In this letter, John frequently addressed his readers as "dear children" (2:1, 12–13, 18, 28; 3:7, 18; 4:4; 5:21; see also 3:1–2, 10; 5:2, 19), an expression of his close bond with them, but also a clear assurance that they were indeed children of God, regardless of the accusations of the false teachers among them. John began here in chapter 3 by reminding them of who they were. He said "behold" or "see" (not translated in the NIV): **How great is the love the Father has lavished on us, that we should be called children of God!** (v. 1). **How great** is literally "of what country," a phrase of astonishment indicating that God's love is completely otherworldly. Its quality is supernatural and incomprehensible. John wanted his readers to understand that it is God's love freely poured out on us through the sacrifice of His Son that makes us children of God, not some secret knowledge. And John's readers were not simply **called children of God** (in name only); they were indeed children of God: **And that is what**

we are! (v. 1; a sentence not included in some ancient manuscripts, but recorded in the oldest and most reliable ones).

The Gnostics didn't acknowledge the Christians' true identity, John said, because they didn't truly know God. It is amazing how many times John used forms of the word *know* in this letter, playing on the Gnostics' claim to have superior knowledge. **The reason the world does not know us is that it did not know him** (v. 1). Not only did the Gnostics not have *superior* knowledge, they didn't even have an *elementary* knowledge of God. It is no wonder, then, that they didn't recognize the true children of God for who they are.

WORDS FROM WESLEY

1 John 3:1

The same invaluable privilege of the sons of God is as strongly asserted by St. John; particularly with regard to the former branch of it, namely, power over outward sin. After he had been crying out, as one astonished at the depth of the riches of the goodness of God—"Behold, what manner of love the Father hath bestowed upon us, that we should be called the sons of God! Beloved, now are we the sons of God: And it doth not yet appear what we shall be; but we know, that when He shall appear, we shall be like Him; for we shall see Him as He is" (1 John 3:1, &c.)—he soon adds, "Whosoever is born of God doth not commit sin; for his seed remaineth in him: And he cannot sin, because he is born of God" (verse 9). But some men will say, "True: Whosoever is born of God doth not commit sin *habitually*." *Habitually!* Whence is that? I read it not. It is not written in the Book. God plainly saith, "He doth not commit sin"; and thou addest, *habitually!* Who art thou that *mendest* the oracles of God?—that "addest to the words of this book"? (WJW, vol. 5, 214–215)

But no doubt some in John's audience were still feeling somewhat inferior to these supposed "super Christians." Maybe they were even wondering if they should be seeking some additional experience to supplement or complete their salvation. John wanted them to understand that the longing in their hearts for something more was (and is) a natural yearning that won't be fully realized until we are with our Lord. He said **what we will be has not yet been made known** (v. 2). We have been given only a glimpse of what awaits us. God has much more in store for His children. One day, in the twinkling of an eye, we will all be changed and raised incorruptible (see 1 Cor. 15:52–54; Phil. 3:21; Rom. 8:18–21). On that day, **when he appears, we shall be like him, for we shall see him as he is** (1 John 3:2). We were created to be like God (Eph. 4:24; Col. 3:4), and, as Christians, our lives are being conformed to the image of God's Son on a daily basis (Rom. 8:29; 1 Cor. 15:49; 2 Cor. 3:4). There is a process to it all that won't be completed until our earthly bodies are transformed. We yearn for that day. And we're assured that it's coming. This is the hope of every believer.

Everyone who has this hope in him (that is, hope in God) **purifies himself, just as he** (Jesus) **is pure** (1 John 3:3). If we are becoming like Him and we know that one day we will see Him face-to-face, does it not stand to reason that we would do everything in our power to imitate Him in this life? Should we not desire to be pure as He is pure (see Lev. 11:44; 1 Pet. 1:15–16; Matt. 5:48)? Peter wrote about the end times, when the world would be destroyed, noting, "Since everything will be destroyed in this way, what kind of people ought you to be? You ought to live holy and godly lives as you look forward to the day of God and speed its coming" (2 Pet. 3:11–12). A belief in the second coming of Christ should motivate us to live godly lives now. Scripture is full of admonitions to purify ourselves (2 Cor. 7:1; 1 Tim. 5:22; James 4:8; 1 Pet. 1:22), indicating that we have a personal responsibility to live a life that is pleasing to God. True children of God want to reflect the character of their heavenly Father.

Children of God Live by the Purpose of the First Coming (1 John 3:4–10)

The Gnostics attempting to lead these Christians astray believed their sinful acts were of no consequence to their spiritual standing, but even false teachers such as these believed that lawlessness (*anomian*, rebellion against God) was evil. The word *sin* used here in 1 John is the Greek word *hamartian*. It has often been defined as "missing the mark," but it should be understood in the context of breaking God's commandments. It's not missing the mark in the sense of being human (and therefore never being able to attain the absolute perfection of God), but in consciously choosing to act in a certain way that misses the mark of God's expectation for us, which is clearly outlined in His Word. Each time you see the verb *sin* in this passage, it translates two Greek verbs. It literally says "to do sin." It is acts of sin that John is talking about, the constant, habitual practice of a lifestyle that is incompatible with Christianity.

The verb "to do" that accompanies "sin" is always used here in some form of the present tense, which the NIV correctly translates by inserting words such as **continues to** or **keeps on** (v. 6). First John 1:9 and 2:1 make it clear that if a Christian commits a sin, there is forgiveness through Christ. But John said, "I write this to you so that you will not sin" (2:1). Christians should never be characterized by sinful lifestyles. An occasional sin is not impossible, but neither should it be inevitable. A lifestyle of continual sin is unthinkable.

WORDS FROM WESLEY

1 John 3:5

Through this faith they are saved from the power of sin, as well as from the guilt of it. So the apostle declares, "Ye know that He was manifested to take away our sins; and in Him is no sin. Whosoever abideth in Him, sinneth not." (WJW, vol. 5, 11)

John wanted the people to know that **sin is lawlessness** (3:4). The two are inseparable and identical. Committing acts of sin is rebellion against God. For Gnostics who were splitting hairs in meaning, John said there is no difference. Missing the mark was tantamount to rebellion against God. And it was evil by anyone's standard.

If John's readers needed a test to determine whether the Gnostics among them were truly Christian, this was it. John was black and white in his description. **No one who lives in him keeps on sinning. No one who continues to sin has either seen him or known him. . . . No one who is born of God will continue to sin . . . he cannot go on sinning, because he has been born of God** (vv. 6, 9). Again, the NIV translates this well. Verse 9 literally says a person is not able to sin, but **to sin** is a present infinitive, which carries the meaning of sinning habitually or, as the NIV renders it, to **go on sinning**. (Note that in 2:1, both verbs are in the aorist tense, which indicates an individual act of sin, not a habitual practice.) John was not saying it is impossible for a Christian to commit a sin, but he was saying it is impossible for a true Christian to choose to live a habitual lifestyle of sin. And he told us why.

John said Jesus came the first time for two very important reasons: **he appeared so that he might take away our sins** (3:5) and **the reason the Son of God appeared was to destroy the devil's work** (v. 8). Jesus didn't come simply to show us a better way to live and love. He didn't come just to let us know how much God loved us; He came to deal with the problem of sin that separated us from a holy God from the time of the fall (Gen. 3). Adam and Eve had been deceived by the serpent, sin entered the world through their disobedience, and every man and woman from that time on has been born into the bondage of sin (Rom. 5:12). But Jesus came to free us from Satan's dominion. He came to destroy the Devil's work (Rom. 6:6; 2 Tim. 1:10; Heb. 2:14).

The verb used here for **destroy** doesn't mean to annihilate, but to loosen the chains that bind us, to render the Devil inoperative, to conquer the Enemy. The Devil's work is to lead us into sin through his lies, but Jesus came to set us free through the truth (see John 8:36, 44). Through His sacrifice, our sins were nailed to the cross, bringing both forgiveness and freedom (see especially Col. 2:13–15). There is victory over sin because Jesus came and died and rose again! If that was His purpose for coming the first time, then we would have to count Him a complete failure if those who are born of Him and who are being conformed to His image are still enslaved to a sinful lifestyle. It is inconceivable. **He is pure** (1 John 3:3); **in him is no sin** (v. 5); **he is righteous** (v. 7). And we're expected to be like Him even now: "Whoever claims to live in him must walk as Jesus did" (1 John 2:6).

WORDS FROM WESLEY

1 John 3:8

He that committeth sin is a child *of the devil: for the devil sinneth from the beginning*—That is, was the first sinner in the universe, and has continued to sin ever since. *The Son of God was manifested to destroy the works of the devil*—All sin. And will He not perform this in all that trust in Him? (ENNT)

Do not let anyone lead you astray (3:7), John warned. All you have to do is look at who Jesus is and what He came to do if you want to recognize who His children are. **He who does what is sinful is of the devil** (v. 8). **This is how we know who the children of God are and who the children of the devil are: Anyone who does not do what is right is not a child of God** (v. 10). If we possess His nature (His **seed** in v. 9; see also 2 Pet. 1:4), then we will display His nature. Our actions and lifestyle will either prove us to be children of God or children of the Devil. There is no in-between for John. You either belong to God and reflect His character, or you belong to the Devil and reflect his. "By their fruit you will recognize them" (Matt. 7:16).

●

WORDS FROM WESLEY

1 John 3:9

But when he is born of God, born of the Spirit, how is the manner of his existence changed! His whole soul is now sensible of God, and he can say, by sure experience, "Thou art about my bed, and about my path"; I feel thee in all my ways: "Thou besettest me behind and before, and layest thy hand upon me." The Spirit or breath of God is immediately inspired, breathed into the new-born soul; and the same breath which comes from, returns to, God: As it is continually received by faith, so it is continually rendered back by love, by prayer, and praise, and thanksgiving; love, and praise, and prayer being the breath of every soul which is truly born of God. And by this new kind of spiritual respiration, spiritual life is not only sustained, but increased day by day, together with spiritual strength, and motion, and sensation; all the senses of the soul being now awake, and capable of discerning spiritual good and evil. (WJW, vol. 5, 226)

DISCUSSION

The evidence is overwhelming that children resemble their biological parents. There is also overwhelming evidence that God's children resemble Him.

1. How does it make you feel to know that God has lavished His love on you?

2. What two glorious future events did John mention in 1 John 3:2?

3. How does the hope of those two events impact your daily life?

4. Do you think a devoted child of God can be popular with the world? Why or why not?

5. What characteristics of Jesus do you find in 1 John 3:3–8?

6. Read 1 John 3:6–10. What distinguishes the lifestyle of a Christian from the lifestyle of a non-Christian? Do you think the distinction is becoming blurry today? Explain.

7. How might you provide clear evidence to an unbeliever that you are God's child?

PRAYER

Father, may our hearts be so filled with Your lavish love that we have no place for sin in our lives.

TRUE OR FALSE?

1 John 4:1–6

_____

Believers discern the validity of spiritual voices and resist false prophets.

After a family relocated to a different state, it searched for a new church home. Upon visiting a nearby church, the parents and their two teenage daughters thought their Sunday school classes were fine, but when the nine-year-old member of the family reported his experience, the family crossed the church off its list. The boy said his Sunday school teacher told the class that Jesus was not the Son of God. He was just a good man, according to the teacher. Further, the teacher instructed his students not to tell the pastor what he had said. "We can't attend this church," the boy concluded. "The teacher doesn't believe the Bible." The boy had tested the teacher's words and judged them to be false.

This study shows us how to test what religious teachers say about Jesus.

COMMENTARY

The book of 1 John was written, in part, to combat false teachers. It was also written to affirm what it means to be a true follower of Christ.

The primary heresy these false teachers were promoting was an early form of Gnosticism. There were a number of streams of Gnosticism. But there were two guiding principles that ran through all Gnostic beliefs. The first principle was that of the supremacy of the intellect. Gnostics would claim to have superior and often hidden knowledge of the truth. What mattered was that they knew these secret "truths." They prided themselves as being the elite of Christendom. If one had this heavenly apprehension of truth, then one need not be bound by ethical constraints. Some Gnostics scandalized the Romans with their behavior, because they believed themselves to be above good and evil.

The second principle of Gnosticism was that spirit was good and matter was evil. If matter is inherently evil, then our physical bodies are evil. If our physical bodies are evil, then it follows that Jesus could not have truly become a person with a physical body because the body is evil. So Jesus couldn't really be human. One solution that was proposed by the Gnostics was to say that Christ really didn't have a body; He only appeared to have a body. What people really saw when they looked at Jesus was some sort of apparition. Another solution to this Gnostic problem was proposed by Cerinthus, who was a resident of Ephesus, like John, though probably later than John. Cerinthus proposed that Jesus be separated from the Christ. He taught that the Christ spirit came upon Jesus following His baptism but left Him before the crucifixion. In teaching this, Cerinthus tried to destroy the idea that God became man at Bethlehem or that Christ died for our sins according to the Scriptures. By holding to Gnostic dogma, he tried to destroy the meaning of both the incarnation and the crucifixion.

It was into this context of incipient Gnosticism that John wrote these words.

Test the Spirits (1 John 4:1–3)

Dear friends, do not believe every spirit, but test the spirits to see whether they are from God (v. 1). Many of us would express these thoughts very differently. We would say, "Test the words of the speaker," or "Do not believe everything that anybody tells you in the name of God, but test the doctrine." But John said to **test the spirits**.

WORDS FROM WESLEY

---

1 John 4:1

Thy hasty servant, Lord, restrain,
Till perfectly renew'd,
As prone alas, to trust in man,
As to mistrust my God!
And lest I every spirit receive
With blind credulity,
Help me each moment to believe
With all my soul in Thee. (PW, vol. 13, 207)

The worldview of the Bible is different from the worldview in North America. Often, Third-World countries have a more biblical worldview. In North America, we each believe, "My thoughts are my thoughts." Therefore, what we do and say, what we build and accomplish, are products of our educations, experiences, personalities, and wills. The biblical worldview says that underneath all of those things is the human spirit that is interacting with both good and evil in the spiritual world that surrounds us. The world of the spirit profoundly influences what we do and say, and what we become.

So when Paul said, "For our struggle is not against flesh and blood, but against the rulers, against the authorities, against the powers of this dark world and against the spiritual forces of evil in the heavenly realms" (Eph. 6:12), he was articulating the same worldview that John was referencing. In a North American worldview, it is people who are a roadblock to God's work. It is warped thinking that begets bad doctrine. It is bad choices that make an immoral life. But John and Paul were saying there is a spiritual reality behind all this.

So John's exhortation is to **test the spirits** (1 John 4:1). What is the spirit behind what is being said? When you hear someone speak, there is a spiritual reality that has influenced what is being said. Is that spiritual reality from God or not?

Danger in the Church (1 John 4:1)

John said that **many false prophets have gone out into the world** (v. 1). The fact that they have **gone out into the world** means they originated in the church. John was less interested in the false philosophies that surrounded him in ancient Rome, because they were outside the church. John was more interested in what was in the church and going out from the church.

False prophets are people who say they speak for God but do not. They say their words are from God but they are not. These people are not speaking by the Spirit of God. John labeled the spirit they are speaking with as an antichrist spirit (4:3). Underneath their choices, philosophies, and perceptions of what is true is an antichrist spirit.

The Tests (1 John 4:2–6)

John then went on to give four tests. These tests will indicate whether a person's speech is influenced by Christ or an antichrist spirit. We will look at these tests as questions.

Question 1. Does the teaching conform to orthodox doctrine (vv. 2–3)?

As was mentioned before, the primary threat to the church was an early form of Gnosticism. In Gnosticism, spirit was good and matter was evil. Therefore, if Jesus was really from God, and God is good, then He could not have come in the flesh. He must have just appeared to be human, but He wasn't really made of matter.

But John said there is a spiritual reality behind that kind of doctrine. It is not from God. It doesn't conform to what we have heard about Jesus. Jesus was real, and anyone who says differently has a spirit that is not from God working behind their words.

John was focused on the problem of Gnosticism. That is why he gave this particular test of orthodoxy. If the problem would have been immorality, the reality of the resurrection, or the nature of God, then the orthodox question may have been different. But the question of John's day was on the nature of Christ. The question is, "What has been said from the beginning" (see 3:11) about these basic question of faith?

When we see people deviating from orthodoxy, there is an **antichrist** (4:3) spirit at work. This is not the end-times Antichrist. This is a spirit that speaks contrary (anti) to what the spirit of Christ has said.

WORDS FROM WESLEY

1 John 4:2

Every spirit—Or teacher, *which confesseth*—Both with heart and voice, *Jesus Christ, who is come in the flesh, is of God*—This His coming presupposes, contains, and draws after it the whole doctrine of Christ. (ENNT)

Question 2. What does your own sense of internal spiritual discernment say (v. 4)?

In 1 John 2:12–14, John talked about the children. They have two characteristics: Their sin has been forgiven, and they know God. In chapter 4, John was saying, "You children are from God. God has done a work in your life. The Spirit of God resides at the core of who you are."

So what happens when their spirits hear the spirit of the antichrist? Even the children, not to mention the young adults and the fathers and mothers of the faith, overcome that spirit. First, they recognize it. There is some sort of disconnect between what they are hearing and what they sense the Spirit of Christ is saying. They become aware of this disconnect and identify that there is something wrong. They recognize the spirit of the antichrist behind what is being said. They don't receive it. They don't believe it. They don't let it undermine their faith. They overcome that spirit.

They overcome because the Spirit of Christ in them is greater than the spirit of the antichrist that is in the world. Notice that this is a spiritual battle. Gnosticism was a doctrinal issue. One of the tests was intellectual: Does it conform to orthodox faith? But there is a spiritual battle to be waged as well.

That spiritual battle is primarily internal. Overcoming the spirit of the antichrist does not necessarily mean winning a debate with one espousing false doctrine. It does not mean winning a political battle within the church. Overcoming means that this false doctrine takes no root in your soul. It does not give a foothold for Satan to destroy your faith. Often when people who are young in the faith face these kinds of difficulties, there is a real battle. Is the Bible true? Can we trust in God's goodness? Battles are OK. But the outcome of the battle should result in the Spirit of Jesus squelching the voice of the antichrist.

Question 3. Is what is being said being received by the world (4:5)?

When something doesn't resonate with your spirit but seems to resonate with people steeped in the spirit of the world, it is a good indication that the spirit that is speaking is not from God.

John said three things about people who speak with the spirit of the antichrist. First, he said they are **from the world** (v. 5). The Bible uses the word *world* in a number of different ways. But here John was referring to a system of thought that either takes no thought of God, or the thoughts they do have of God spring from how they have imagined Him to be and not how God has revealed himself.

John said that because these people come from the world, they take the world's viewpoint. They take as true what the world says about who we are and who God is.

The third thing John said about them is that **the world listens to them** (v. 5). What is being said is coming out of the world's frame of reference. It affirms what they see to be true, and so it resonates with what they think.

There are times when, because of a movement of the Spirit or the favor of God, the world sees the truth that is in the gospel. But this is not the way things usually are. So whenever the world is resonating with what is being said, be suspicious.

WORDS FROM WESLEY

1 John 4:5

They—Those false prophets, *are of the world*—Of the number of those that know not God: *therefore speak they of the world*—From the same principle, wisdom, spirit, and of consequence *the world heareth them*—With approbation. (ENNT)

Question 4. Does it conform to the teaching of the apostles (4:6)?

John—as an apostle called by Jesus, filled with the Spirit, and affirmed by the church—said **we are from God** (v. 6). The church has always been built on the shoulders of the apostles. The New Testament was written by either the apostles or people tutored by the apostles (for example, Mark and Luke).

John said that if people know God, then what the apostles say will not only resonate in their spirits, but these individuals will also recognize the authority of their words. People who know God will follow the words of the apostles. People who do not know God will not listen to the apostles and will not view their words as authoritative. This is close to the question about orthodoxy. However, it is a narrower question. Orthodoxy has to do with their view of the whole canon of Scripture, from Moses to the Prophets to the words of Jesus. What the apostles had testified to was their experience with Jesus.

WORDS FROM WESLEY

1 John 4:6

Lift up, therefore, your heart to the Spirit of truth, and beg of Him to shine upon it, that, without respecting any man's person, you may see and follow the truth as it is in Jesus. (WJW, vol. 7, 69)

The Gnostics viewed themselves as spiritual people. But they thought their own philosophy of the world was more authoritative than what the apostle said. We have many people in our world who claim to be spiritual, but their spirituality is based on their own terms. They define who God is, what truth is, what morality looks like, and what it looks like to be spiritual. But without submitting to the authority of what the apostles said, they show themselves to not know God.

The command in this passage is to test the spirits. We need to know what is from God.

DISCUSSION

False teaching abounds, and believers must proactively oppose it. The litmus test for identifying false teaching is the biblical truth about Jesus Christ.

1. What forms of Gnosticism do you see today?

2. How does the worldview of the Bible differ in Third-World countries from that of North America?

3. Why do you agree or disagree that bad choices make an immoral life?

4. How do you account for the fact that so many false teachers used to belong to a biblically sound church?

5. How do you account for religious liberalism in a denomination that had previously adhered to the truth?

6. What tests did John give for identifying the spirit of antichrist?

7. What kinds of religious teachings are popular with the world?

PRAYER

Father, guard our hearts from untruth, and give us the clarity, wisdom, and knowledge to stand against it.

THE SOURCE OF ALL LOVE

1 John 4:7–21

God's love is the source and standard of love manifested through us.

John Fawcett, the author of the hymn "Blest Be the Tie That Binds," accepted a call in 1772 to become pastor of a famous church in London, England. However, as he loaded his goods onto a wagon and was ready to leave the small country church he had served for seven years, the people of the church surrounded the wagon. Tearfully, they expressed the sorrow they felt because he was leaving. John was so moved by the church family's display of love that he unpacked his goods and notified the London church that he had decided not to become its pastor. The next week, he wrote: "Blest be the tie that binds our hearts in Christian love." He stayed at the country church the rest of his life.

This study will illuminate our hearts and minds with the true meaning of God's love and our love for one another.

COMMENTARY

God is love. John wanted to be sure this teaching was clear. Throughout 1 John, he presented his case that God is love, Jesus Christ is the gift of that love, and abiding in God through Jesus is the result of God's love in and through us.

First John 3:23 provides context for this study's passage: "And this is his command: to believe in the name of his Son, Jesus Christ, and to love one another as he commanded us." The first half of this command—"to believe in the name of his Son"—is discussed in the first seven verses of chapter 4. Verses 7–21 are the extension of the second half of the command—"to love one another as he commanded us."

We Love Because We Have Been Loved by God (1 John 4:7–11)

John made it clear that all our ability to love one another comes from God's love in us, **for love comes from God** (v. 7). This fact is the whole premise of loving one another. John further illustrated the extent of God's love with language similar to the words of Jesus to Nicodemus: **This is how God showed his love among us: He sent his one and only Son into the world that we might live through him** (v. 9).

What does this love really mean? After all, we love our neighbors differently than we love our spouses or children. We are to love our neighbors with God's unconditional and perfect love. This love is based on the character of the lover and not on the object of that love. God doesn't love us because of what we have done for Him; God loves us because in His nature, **God is love** (v. 8).

Therefore, **whoever does not love does not know God** (v. 8). If we know God—that is, we have believed in the name of His Son, Jesus Christ (3:23)—then God's nature will flow in and through our nature. His love will infuse our nature and be evident in our lives.

WORDS FROM WESLEY

1 John 4:8

God is love—This little sentence brought St. John more sweetness, even in the time he was writing it, than the whole world can bring. God is often styled holy, righteous, wise: but not holiness, righteousness, or wisdom in the abstract: as He is said to be love: intimating that this is His darling, His reigning attribute; the attribute that sheds an amiable glory on all His other perfections. (ENNT)

John went to great lengths to demonstrate the measure of God's intense love. **This is love: not that we loved God, but that he loved us and sent his Son as an atoning sacrifice for our sins** (v. 10). If it weren't for God's love manifest in the sacrifice of Jesus Christ, we would be lost and enslaved to sin and hatred. We don't have the ability to love on our own; only God's love in us allows us to love each other.

WORDS FROM WESLEY

1 John 4:10

And herein "was the love of God manifested towards us, that he sent his Son to be the propitiation for our sins" (1 John 4:9–10). So was the Lord "our righteousness" (Jer. 23:6); without which we could not have been justified. As man owed his Creator the perfect obedience of his whole life, or a punishment proportioned to his transgression, it was impossible he could satisfy Him by a partial and imperfect obedience. Neither could he merit anything from Him to whom he owed all things. There was need therefore of a Mediator who could repair the immense wrong he had done to the Divine Majesty, satisfy the Supreme Judge, who had pronounced the sentence of death against the transgressors of His law, suffer in the place of His people, and merit for them pardon, holiness, and glory. (WJW, vol. 9, 489–490)

What does it mean that Christ was sent **as an atoning sacrifice for our sins**? For believers, this means everything. Since the fall in Genesis 3, there has been a chasm between holy God and sinful people. Through Moses, God established the sacrificial system in which the shed blood of animals atoned—or covered over—human sin. As one of the sacrificial practices, a scapegoat would be released into the wilderness on the Day of Atonement to symbolize the removal of sin "as far as the east is from the west" (Ps. 103:12).

God instituted the sacrifices and the Day of Atonement, but they were only meant to temporarily care for the problem of sin. They served as a tool to instruct God's people of what the Messiah would one day do. When Christ came, He came as "the Lamb of God, who takes away the sin of the world" (John 1:29). Through the blood of Jesus, our sins aren't just covered; they are completely removed. The forgiveness of our sin is the outcome of God's love-gift, Jesus Christ. His forgiveness is a direct result of God's love for us. He loves the world so much that He gave His Son to tear down that barrier between us and God.

"How great is the love the Father has lavished on us, that we should be called children of God!" (1 John 3:1). This love that the Father has lavished on us through the sacrificial gift of His Son is the basis of John's statement, **since God so loved us, we also ought to love one another** (4:11).

Love Is Complete When We Are in Him (1 John 4:12–18)

When we live out the love of God in our lives, **his love is made complete in us** (v. 12). In the English translation, we may lose some of John's intended meaning here. In the Greek, the tense would correctly be translated "His love is *being made* complete in us." This is a continual process; it will not be achieved in this lifetime. We always have room to grow.

Yet we have the promise that we can **know that we live in him and he in us, because he has given us of his Spirit** (v. 13). John stated that he knew because he had seen with his own eyes. He was an eyewitness of the love of God manifest in Jesus Christ. On the evening before His death, Jesus used very similar words in His teaching to the disciples: "Remain in me, and I will remain in you" (John 15:4). **We have seen and testify** (1 John 4:14) that all this happened and it is true, John said.

John noted two primary conditions to the testimony of God's abiding presence. First, **if we love one another, God lives in us** (v. 12). To love one another is to reveal His presence through our lives. To truly love one another requires His presence because we are incapable of doing so on our own.

Second, **if anyone acknowledges that Jesus is the Son of God, God lives in him and he in God** (v. 15). This acknowledgment is not merely intellectual consent—that is, we believe God exists. After all, James said, "even the demons believe that" (James 2:19). This acknowledgment is also heart consent through genuine belief and trust. To truly acknowledge Jesus as Son of God is to believe in His atoning work, to receive His love, and to obey His commands.

We can **know and rely on the love God has for us** (1 John 4:16) by the confirmation of His work in our lives. This love of God will continually grow in our lives through reading His Word, praying, and living in community with others. We can rely on the love God has for us because His love is manifest through other believers.

God is love (v. 16). His very essence, nature, and community within himself is found in the character of love. Beyond His holiness, justice, and grace is His love.

WORDS FROM WESLEY

1 John 4:17

Thus doth Jesus "save His people from their sins:" And not only from outward sins, but also from the sins of their hearts; from evil thoughts, and from evil tempers—"True," say some, "we shall thus be saved from our sins; but not till death; not in this world." But how are we to reconcile this with the express words of St. John?— "Herein is our love made perfect, that we may have boldness in the day of judgment. Because as He is, so are we in this world." The apostle here, beyond all contradiction, speaks of himself and other living Christians, of whom (as though he had foreseen this very evasion, and set himself to overturn it from the foundation) he flatly affirms, that not only at or after death, but *in this world*, they are as their Master (1 John 4:17). (WJW, vol. 6, 18)

Now, we must treat the topic of *how* to abide in Him. How can we know God and His love if we do not spend time with Him? How can we bear fruit if we are not intimately connected with the Vine, which is the source of this love? How can we **have confidence on the day of judgment** (v. 17) if we are afraid of Him?

Although God is love, our love for one another is not natural or automatic with becoming a child of God. We must spend time with Him through the Word and prayer, **because in this world we are like him** (v. 17). We are God's ambassadors (2 Cor. 5:20). What the world knows about us, it knows about God. We must be careful to live in God's love so as to reveal who He truly is.

For believers, the idea that we are ambassadors and representatives of God in the world might strike fear in our hearts, but John wrote, **There is no fear in love. But perfect love drives out fear** (1 John 4:18). Fear and love for God and one another are incompatible. **The one who fears is not made perfect in love** (v. 18). To be made perfect in love is to continually grow more in love with the Father through Christ—to fall in love deeper and deeper, like we learn to love our spouse or children more deeply.

WORDS FROM WESLEY
1 John 4:18

There is no fear in love—No slavish fear can be where love reigns; *but perfect*, adult *love casteth out* slavish *fear; because* such *fear hath torment*, and so is inconsistent with the happiness of love. A natural man has neither fear, nor love: one that is awakened, fear without love; a babe in Christ, love and fear; a father in Christ, love without fear. (ENNT)

We Love Because God First Loved Us (1 John 4:19–21)

These truths about the depth of God's love in Christ lead to the climax of John's thoughts in verse 19: **We love because he first loved us**. Our love for one another comes directly from God. To consider the extent of God's love would require volumes of writing; then, we probably would still miss something. God loves His children so much that it is beyond human comprehension. Human love is often shallow and fleeting; one betrayal of trust or action of resentment and our love fails. Yet God's love never fails. It is patient, kind, and doesn't keep record of wrongs. God's love protects, trusts, and perseveres, even when our actions don't deserve it (1 Cor. 13). Human love is oftentimes based on selfish desires—we first look to see what we can get out of the relationship. God's love is others-focused; it is about how He can give to us. His love is about how He can better our lives. His love was shown in its fullness when Christ extended His hands and allowed himself to be crucified for our sins. Humanity didn't deserve His love, but He gave it freely because of who He is.

Thinking about the extent of God's love through Christ, we must again consider John's words: **We love because he first loved us** (4:19). What does our love for other people look like? Are we selfish or selfless? Are we in it for our own benefit or for the benefit of others? Do we love others out of gratefulness for Christ's love, for what we can gain from loving them, or because we fear the consequences of not doing so?

It is sad how God's church has earned a poor reputation from professing believers who do evil things "in the name of Christ." True believers are not going to hate people because of their nationality, race, or lifestyle. They are not going to be hurtful or cruel to people who are sinful; true believers will "love the sinner and hate the sin." **If anyone says, "I love God," yet hates his brother, he is a liar** (v. 20). Why would John call these people liars? God's love naturally manifests itself through true believers in the form of love for one another. Love for one another is impossible on our own, but if "we live in him and he in us" (4:13), then we will love each other.

John used the argument that it is much more difficult to love what we have not seen than what we have seen; thus, **anyone who does not love his brother, whom he has seen, cannot love God, whom he has not seen** (v. 20). We know God only through the testimony of His Word and the Holy Spirit within; we can know our brother or sister by sharing life. There is a huge difference. When we share life, bonds of love are natural to form. When we spend time with one another, we learn to love one another. When we suffer or rejoice together, when we pray and worship with one another, there is a bond of love that develops that is like no other.

Loving God, on the other hand, is an issue of great faith. We have not seen God; we have only heard about Him. Yes, we have His Word and we have the testimony of saints past and present, but our experiences of God is through faith. We cannot know God unless we possess faith in God.

The bottom line is this: **Whoever loves God must also love his brother** (v. 21). This is the greatest evidence of a believer's love.

DISCUSSION

God demonstrated the kind of love He wants us to practice.

1. Is God's love conditional or unconditional? Defend your answer.

2. Why do you agree or disagree that you cannot love others until first you love yourself?

3. What is your opinion of the statement, "I love you in the Lord"?

4. Read Galatians 2:20. How does Jesus' love for us inspire us to live for Him?

5. What tests of our identification with God do you find in 1 John 4:13–16?

6. Do you think God created human beings because He needed someone to love? Why or why not?

7. What wrong message about God's love might a church disagreement send to unbelievers?

8. How might a church demonstrate God's love in practical ways?

PRAYER

Lord, thank You for loving us long before we came to love You. Help us to love others with a little more of Your love today.

THREE SPIRITUAL TRUTHS

1 John 5:1–12

Those who are "born of God" overcome the world.

Relativism has become quite popular. It is a philosophy that claims there is no absolute truth—everything is relative. It is a handy excuse for believing whatever one wants to believe and for doing whatever one chooses to do. Relativism rejects the Bible as absolute truth; therefore the relativist sees no higher authority than self for deciding right from wrong. In relativist thinking, no one can legitimately judge because there is no absolute standard for determining right from wrong.

This study focuses on absolute truths that merit our full confidence.

COMMENTARY

The gospel of John is often called the "Gospel of Belief." The theme of the book is summarized in John 20:31: "But these are written that you may believe that Jesus is the Christ, the Son of God, and that by believing you may have life in his name." John mentioned various people who believed and told how the "signs" (miracles) Jesus performed produced belief in people who saw them. Writing in 1 John, the apostle also emphasized the importance of belief, for belief was commanded and belief was the key to being born of God (3:23; 5:1). However, belief must also be discriminating because there are many false prophets who have gone out into the world (4:1). Affirming true belief in Jesus Christ and countering false teachings are major themes throughout 1 John.

Tradition favors a late date for the writing of 1 John, perhaps A.D. 90 or later. Along with several other canonical Epistles that were written later in the New Testament period, 1 John shows great concern about the threat of false prophets. Colossians, 1 and 2 Timothy, Titus, 1 and 2 Peter, Jude, and the three epistles of John all have sections warning about the threat of false teachings and false teachers. People then and now often seem interested and gullible when it comes to false teaching.

Gnosticism was apparently beginning to be a threat to Christian teaching even in the first century. The period when the Gnostic threat to Christian teaching was the most serious came later, during the second and third centuries. Most of our information about Gnosticism comes from that later period. The Gnostic teachers were never very organized or unified in their ideas, and they might be compared to New Age advocates today. Some common Gnostic ideas can be identified, however. Gnostics believed that salvation was through special knowledge. (In Greek the word for knowledge is *gnosis*.) Matter, including the body, was considered the source of evil, but spirit was good.

Believing the body is the source of evil, some Gnostic teachers taught that since Jesus was divine, He could not have really had a human body. Some suggested that He just "appeared" to have a body. First John 1:1 may address that idea directly. Several times throughout the letter John affirmed that Jesus is the Christ who came in the flesh (1:1–4; 2:22; 4:2–3, 15; 5:1, 5). He drove that point home, apparently in opposition to teachers who had denied that fact. Other Gnostics taught that Jesus was born as a man and became divine at His baptism only to have the divine nature leave Him before His death on the cross. This teaching may be what John was addressing in 1 John 5:1–12.

In contrast to the false prophets, however, John said he was writing about things he knew. He had personal experience with Jesus. "That which was from the beginning, which we have heard, which we have seen with our eyes, which we have looked at and our hands have touched—this we proclaim concerning the Word of life" (1 John 1:1). John said he was not speculating or writing information from others; rather, he wrote about what he had experienced for himself.

Believe That Jesus Is the Christ (1 John 5:1–2)

John knew personally that Jesus is the Christ or Messiah who had come in the flesh. But more important than simply having knowledge is the fact that everyone who believes is born of God. Faith provides the access to the new birth—a message affirmed throughout the New Testament.

●

WORDS FROM WESLEY

1 John 5:1

The true, living, Christian faith, which whosoever hath, is born of God, is not only assent, an act of the understanding; but a disposition, which God hath wrought in his heart; "a sure trust and confidence in God, that, through the merits of Christ, his sins are forgiven, and he reconciled to the favour of God." This implies, that a man first renounce himself; that, in order to be "found in Christ," to be accepted through Him, he totally rejects all "confidence in the flesh"; that, "having nothing to pay," having no trust in his own works or righteousness of any kind, he comes to God as a lost, miserable, self-destroyed, self-condemned, undone, help-less sinner; as one whose mouth is utterly stopped, and who is alto-gether "guilty before God." Such a sense of sin (commonly called despair, by those who speak evil of the things they know not), together with a full conviction, such as no words can express, that of Christ only cometh our salvation, and an earnest desire of that salvation, must precede a living faith, a trust in Him, who "for us paid our ransom by his death, and fulfilled the law in his life." This faith then, whereby we are born of God, is "not only a belief of all the articles of our faith, but also a true confidence of the mercy of God, through our Lord Jesus Christ." (WJW, vol. 5, 213–214)

Another theme that permeates this letter is love. In an age of strong family ties, John told us that **everyone who loves the father loves his child as well** (v. 1). Loving God opens us to loving all God's children. **This is how we know that we love the children of God: by loving God and carrying out his commands** (v. 2). Through loving God and obeying His commands, we will show our love for His children. A logical equivalent would be that if we do not love God's children, then we do not love God. How do we show love to God's children? By feeding the hungry, clothing the naked, caring for the orphans, and visiting the prisoners (Matt. 25:37–40). Or as John himself said, we should lay down our lives for our brothers and sisters, and we most certainly should share our plenty with the one who is in need (1 John 3:16–18).

Everyone Born of God Overcomes the World (1 John 5:3–5)

God's **commands are not burdensome** (v. 3). God promises His children that they will not be left on their own as they walk with Him. He will strengthen and aid them as they live the Christian life. Centuries before this letter, Jeremiah had stated God's promise of a new covenant: "I will put my law in their minds and write it on their hearts. I will be their God, and they will be my people" (Jer. 31:33). Jeremiah promised an internal change in God's people. In his gospel, John quoted Jesus as promising to ask the Father to send the Holy Spirit to aid His followers: "I will ask the Father, and he will give you another Counselor to be with you forever—the Spirit of truth" (John 14:16–17). Walking with God is not always an easy way, but with the aid of the Holy Spirit, we can succeed. And not only do we succeed, we also find God's way always turns out to be the best way—**his commands are not burdensome** (1 John 5:3).

WORDS FROM WESLEY

1 John 5:4

For whatsoever—This expression implies the most unlimited universality, *is born of God overcometh the world*—Conquers whatever it can lay in the way, either to allure or fright the children of God from keeping His commandments. *And this is the victory*—The grand means of overcoming, *even our faith*—seeing all things are possible to him that believeth. (ENNT)

Obeying God's commands means we are not conformed to the world and its ways. **For everyone born of God overcomes the world. This is the victory that has overcome the world, even our faith** (v. 4). As children of God, our lives do not follow the pattern of the world and its evil ways. Through the aid of the Holy Spirit, we overcome the world as we keep God's commands. The key to our overcoming is our faith in Jesus. **Who is it that overcomes the world? Only he who believes that Jesus is the Son of God** (v. 5). John returned to his theme that Jesus is the divine Messiah, the Son of God.

John emphasized that our faith in Jesus must make a difference in our lives. Belief produces love for God; love for God produces love for God's children; love causes us to obey God's commands; we are enabled to obey God's commands through our faith in Jesus. Love, faith, and obedience are linked together in the life of the believer.

WORDS FROM WESLEY

1 John 5:5

Who is he that overcometh the world?—That is superior to all worldly care, desire, fear? Every believer, and none else. (ENNT)

Three That Testify: Spirit, Water, and Blood (1 John 5:6–8)

In the ancient world, the testimony of multiple witnesses was considered necessary if a testimony was questioned. This is illustrated in Jesus' life when the Pharisees challenged Him about His claims, saying that He was His own witness. Jesus replied that the Father was a second witness to His personal claims (John 8:12–18). In this first letter, John claimed that Jesus is indeed God come in the flesh and cited three witnesses to support his claim: (1) Jesus' water baptism, (2) Jesus' shed blood when He died on the cross, and (3) the Spirit's witness to Jesus. Furthermore, the Spirit witnessed in two ways—when He descended as a dove at the baptism of Jesus and when He witnesses in the hearts of believers. John reiterated that the Spirit is the truth, words of Jesus he had also quoted in his gospel. "When the Counselor comes, whom I will send to you from the Father, the Spirit of truth who goes out from the Father, he will testify about me" (John 15:26).

In this passage, John may have been arguing against those Gnostics who claimed the divinity of Jesus lasted only between the time of His baptism and the time of His death. The three witnesses testify, and they agree on what they say, providing still more credible proof that Jesus Christ is God who has come in the flesh.

The Testimony of God (1 John 5:9–10)

John paused to affirm the importance of the Spirit's witness. We accept human testimony related to many things. But the testimony of the Spirit is much more important. How wonderful to know within our hearts that we have been born again. Nothing can compare to the inner witness of the Spirit; nor can anything replace that assurance that we are indeed children of God. We do not have to wonder about our relationship to God; for in our hearts the Spirit gives us assurance that we are God's children when we believe in Jesus, the Son of God.

God Has Given Us Eternal Life (1 John 5:11–12)

What is the testimony the Spirit gives us? John spelled it out once again: (1) **God has given us eternal life**; (2) eternal life comes through Jesus Christ, His Son; (3) if we have **the Son**, we have **life**; and (4) if we do **not have the Son of God**, we do **not have life** (vv. 11–12). Gnostics may talk about special knowledge that leads to salvation for the spiritual elite. John said the only knowledge we need is knowledge that is open to all: Jesus is the Son of God, and He brings eternal life to all who believe in Him. No other way is provided for us to have the eternal life that God has freely offered. The good news is that this way is open to "anyone who believes" (v. 10).

WORDS FROM WESLEY

1 John 5:11

And this is the sum of that testimony, that God hath given us a title to, and the real beginning of, eternal life: And that this is purchased by, and treasured up in His Son, who has all the springs and the fullness of it in himself, to communicate to His body the church, first in grace, and then in glory. (ENNT)

DISCUSSION

Our faith stands on the One who himself is truth, not on human speculations or vain philosophies. What we believe about Jesus Christ must be anchored in a personal relationship with Him.

1. Why do you agree or disagree that Gnosticism and New Age philosophy are similar?

2. What does it mean to believe that Jesus is the Christ (1 John 5:1)?

3. According to 1 John 5:1–2, how can we be sure we are born of God?

4. How would you answer someone who says he or she would like to become a Christian but is afraid that he or she wouldn't be able to keep God's commandments? See 1 John 5:3.

5. How does the Holy Spirit help believers keep the Lord's commandments?

6. How are love, faith, and obedience linked together in the life of a believer?

7. Based on 1 John 5:11–12, how do you know no one can earn eternal life?

8. Why do you agree or disagree that we cannot know we have eternal life until we die?

PRAYER

Father, thank You that loving You is as simple as keeping Your commands. Help us to do that today.

9

PRAYING WITH CONFIDENCE

1 John 5:13–21

Christians are confident in God through Jesus Christ.

A new word, *Tebowing*, slipped into the English language when Tim Tebow, former quarterback for the Denver Broncos, knelt for prayer on the sidelines. The media and football fans were soon buzzing about Tebowing. But many fans did more than speak the word; they also imitated the prayer posture. Tebowing became a cultural fad. But kneeling like Tim Tebow doesn't mean the person in that position is actually praying. God associates real prayer—effective prayer—with spiritual posture, an attitude of the heart that reaches out to Him with confidence and in submission to His will.

This study expands our understanding of effective prayer and motivates us to approach God with the right attitude.

COMMENTARY

The previous study ended with a strong affirmation that eternal life is given to those who believe in the Son of God (1 John 5:11–12). John was opposing those who taught that Jesus Christ did not really come in the flesh, or that Jesus was a man who was only united with divinity during the time between His baptism and crucifixion. Instead, in his first letter, John told us repeatedly that Jesus Christ has come in the flesh. In fact, John called the one who denies that fact the antichrist (2:22). In his first letter, John appeared to have been very concerned about false teaching that was typical of Gnosticism.

This Gnosticism was from the same milieu that produced the Nag Hammadi library, discovered in Egypt in the late 1940s. This collection of documents is well-known to scholars and was made famous (or infamous) by Dan Brown's book, *The Da Vinci Code*. Most of the Gnostic writings known to modern scholars date from the second or third century and were produced by writers who were deemed heretical in the early church. From the concerns John expressed, he seemed to have encountered teachings from those Gnostic teachers, perhaps in an early form. He warned his readers against some specific teachings and urged them to "test the spirits to see whether they are from God" (4:1). In spite of confusion spread by false teachers, Gnostic or otherwise, John assured his readers that they could be confident in believing "in the name of the Son of God" (5:13).

Know That You Have Eternal Life (1 John 5:13)

The Gnostics claimed to have special knowledge that could be known by a few elite followers. As an apostle of Jesus, John witnessed to the fact that believers can know they have eternal life, but it doesn't come through secret knowledge. They can know they have eternal life if they believe in the name of Jesus. There is nothing esoteric or secret about it. The gospel is for everyone, and everyone can believe it if they will. As in his gospel, John wrote with the purpose of leading the readers to believe.

Luke told us that as Jesus ascended into the heavens, the apostles were commissioned to be His witnesses (Acts 1:8). Now as John wrote this letter, it was some six decades later. John knew he would not be around to give a verbal witness for much longer. He wanted the readers to be assured of their faith in Jesus and not confused by false knowledge that was being taught by the Gnostics or others like them. Earlier, the apostle Peter had written in much the same way. Some three decades before, Peter had written that he wanted to confirm believers in their faith because his death was imminent (2 Pet. 1:12–18). The apostolic witness to Jesus was considered important in New Testament times; today, it is still important.

WORDS FROM WESLEY

1 John 5:13

These things have I written—In the introduction (ch. 1:4) he said, I write; now, in the close, I have written; *that ye may know*—With a fuller and stronger assurance, that ye have eternal life. (ENNT)

Ask According to God's Will and He Will Answer (1 John 5:14–15)

John already stated that we can know we have eternal life. He assured us that we can have confidence in God for our day-to-day living as well. We express our desires to God in prayer, knowing He will answer according to His will. Prayer is our expression of dependence on and confidence in God. Whenever we know something is God's will, we can ask, believing that He hears us and will answer us. Many times we are uncertain of God's will, but we should always pray for it to be done. We can pray in complete confidence that He hears, and, if He hears, we have—according to His will—what we asked of Him. We should live prayerfully, always acknowledging our dependence on God and knowing that He hears our prayers and cares for us.

If Anyone Sees His Brother Commit a Sin, He Should Pray (1 John 5:16–17)

John illustrated the kind of prayer we should pray, knowing that our request is according to God's will. We should pray for any brother or sister who commits a sin. This is a rather difficult passage to understand. John distinguished sins that lead to death from sins that do not lead to death. Perhaps John was referring to Gnostic teaching that denied the incarnation as the sin that leads to death. Surely it is true that as anyone persists in false teaching and immorality, his or her doom is sealed—such sin leads to death.

Whatever John meant by the **sin that leads to death** (v. 16), assuredly he appears to have distinguished between various kinds of sins. **All wrongdoing is sin, and there is sin that does not lead to death** (v. 17). Theologians distinguish at least three meanings for the word *sin*. First, there is sin in the broadest sense of missing the mark or missing God's perfect will. All of us fall short of that perfect goal throughout our lives. Thus, we all sin in that sense. Second, there is also the sin of rebellion by which one sets him- or herself against God and His will for us. Last, there is, as John Wesley noted, sin as a willful transgression of a known law of God. We believe it is possible to be delivered from sin in the second and third senses, and sin in the first sense is covered by the atonement of Christ. Also as we study the Bible, it seems that the only sin that cannot be forgiven is the sin for which a person is not repentant; that is, the person is not willing to turn from the sin. All sin is forgiven through the atonement of Christ if the sinner repents and trusts Jesus.

So what did John mean by the **sin that leads to death** (v. 16)? John's exact meaning is unclear. But, sadly, John seemed to have been saying that there are some people who are beyond the reach of our prayers. The antichrists John described in 2:18–23 were former believers who had turned from the truth of the incarnation. Perhaps that is the sin that leads to death. John did not forbid us to pray for those caught in this sin. He simply seemed to have had little or no hope of those prayers being effective.

The One Born of God (1 John 5:18)

John stated three things we know in 5:18–20. First, John, like Paul, clearly stated that the person who is born again is a changed individual. No longer does the born-again believer follow the ways of this sinful world by living a life of sin. The believer is changed by the power of Jesus, and **the one who was born of God** (Jesus) **keeps him** (the believer) **safe** from **the evil one** (v. 18). We are never left alone in the struggle with evil. The English Standard Version translates verse 18 this way: "Everyone who has been born of God does not keep on sinning, but he who was born of God protects him, and the evil one does not touch him." Can the believer sin? Yes. Can the believer live above willful, habitual sin? Yes. Through the power of the Holy Spirit victory over sin is ours if we trust in Jesus. John's words are very forceful—the believer **does not continue to sin** (v. 18). Through the atonement, Jesus has provided power for us to live above sin and defeat.

WORDS FROM WESLEY

1 John 5:18

He that is, by faith, born of God, sinneth not (1) by any habitual sin; for all habitual sin is sin reigning: But sin cannot reign in any that believeth. Nor (2) by any willful sin; for his will, while he abideth in the faith, is utterly set against all sin, and abhorreth it as deadly poison. Nor (3) by any sinful desire; for he continually desireth the holy and perfect will of God; and any tendency to an unholy desire, he, by the grace of God, stifleth in the birth. Nor (4) doth he sin by infirmities, whether in act, word, or thought; for his infirmities have no concurrence of his will; and without this they are not properly sins. Thus, "he that is born of God doth not commit sin": And though he cannot say, he hath not sinned, yet now "he sinneth not." (WJW, vol. 5, 11)

We Know We Are Children of God (1 John 5:19)

How sad it is that the children of God frequently mimic the **world** that **is under the control of the evil one** (v. 19). John agreed with Paul's words in Romans: "Do not conform any longer to the pattern of this world, but be transformed by the renewing of your mind" (Rom. 12:2). John was methodical in his approach: (1) We know we are born of God; (2) we know those who are born of God do not continue to sin; (3) we know Jesus protects us from the Evil One; and (4) we know the world is controlled by the Evil One. Thus, the unstated conclusion is that we should certainly not mimic the world in its sin. John had already declared, "If anyone loves the world, the love of the Father is not in him" (1 John 2:15). We are called to something better than the world has to offer. May God help us to live like children of God and not to live like the world portrays "the good life."

WORDS FROM WESLEY

1 John 5:19

Consider likewise 1 John 5:19: "We know that we are of God." How? "By the Spirit that He hath given us." Nay, "hereby we know that He abideth in us." And what ground have we, either from Scripture or reason, to exclude the witness, any more than the fruit, of the Spirit, from being here intended? By this then also "we know that we are of God," and in what sense we are so; whether we are babes, young men, or fathers, we know in the same manner.

Not that I affirm that all young men, or even fathers, have this testimony every moment. There may be intermissions of the direct testimony that they are thus born of God; but those intermissions are fewer and shorter as they grow up in Christ; and some have the testimony both of their justification and sanctification, without any intermission at all; which I presume more might have, did they walk humbly and closely with God. (WJW, vol. 11, 421)

Jesus Christ Is the True God and Eternal Life (1 John 5:20)

This is the last of the three things in 5:18–20 that John said we know. Verses 18–20 summarize much of what John wrote throughout the letter. In this verse, he moved back to his main point: **We know also that the Son of God has come** (v. 20). We know the truth. True knowledge was promised by the Gnostics, but they could not deliver what they promised. John promised an alternative that is much better than that promised by the false prophets. In Christ believers are in the truth. In Christ they are in eternal life.

Keep Yourselves from Idols (1 John 5:21)

As his closing statement, John exhorted his **dear children** (v. 21) to avoid idols. In light of his letter, the idols he had in mind may be false beliefs. He already said anything that is of the world is of the Evil One. An idol, then, may be anything of the world that comes between us and God. Reason, ambition, false doctrine, self, other persons, or material goods can all become idols. John keenly recognized that we easily fall prey to idolatry and warned against such failure. As he said in verse 18, Jesus keeps us safe from the Evil One, but Jesus does not take us out of this world where idols abound. We still can choose those idols. May God help us in this day of material abundance that we will keep ourselves from idols.

WORDS FROM WESLEY
1 John 5:21

An ancient historian relates, that when the apostle was so enfeebled by age as not to be able to preach, he was frequently brought into the congregation in his chair, and just uttered, "Beloved children, love one another." He could not have given a more important advice. And equally important is this which lies before us; equally necessary for every part of the church of Christ. "Beloved children, keep yourselves from idols."

Indeed there is a close connection between them: One cannot subsist without the other. As there is no firm foundation for the love of our brethren except the love of God, so there is no possibility of loving God except we keep ourselves from idols. (WJW, vol. 6, 435)

DISCUSSION

Prayer is a powerful device that God has given for our good and His glory. When we pray, we should be confident that He hears and answers us.

1. The first-century Gnostics believed they had secret knowledge, but what extraordinary, genuine knowledge do believers have, according to 1 John 5:13? Why would it be wrong to keep this knowledge secret?

2. Why is it wrong to pray with an I-hope-God-will-hear-me attitude?

3. What helps you determine that what you ask for in prayer is God's will for you?

4. Why do you agree or disagree that "Wait" is often an unwelcome answer to prayer? How has it proven to be the right answer to prayer for you?

5. What do you think is meant by "a sin that leads to death" (1 John 5:16)?

6. Do you think it is right to assume that a person was never born again if there is no evidence that his or her life has changed? Defend your answer.

7. What idols do you think some Christians worship? How can we keep ourselves from idols?

PRAYER

Father, thank You that through Your Spirit we can overcome sin. And thank You that when we ask anything according to Your will, You will hear.

WHAT A JOURNEY!

2 John 1–13

Christians walk in the truth, obedience, and love.

A story, perhaps unsubstantiated, reports that two church officers were so impressed with their pastor's holy life that they suspected he prayed for hours before getting into bed. They conspired to slip into the old preacher's unlocked home and hide under his bed to spy on his nightly prayer habit. To their great surprise, when their elderly pastor arrived and knelt by his bed, he offered just a brief prayer: "Good night, Lord. It's been a wonderful day."

We may not approve of such a brief prayer, but we must approve of wonderful daily walks with the Lord. This study equips us for walks with the Lord every day of our spiritual journey.

COMMENTARY

John's three epistles, along with the gospel of John, show so many similarities in writing style that it is virtually without question that the same writer penned all four. John needed only identify himself as "the elder" (2 John 1), not merely a reference to his age, but more probably to the position he held in the church (see Acts 20:17; Titus 1:5; 1 Pet. 5:1 for similar uses of the Greek term *presbyteros*). John was ministering in Asia Minor at this time, and was responsible for a number of churches in and around the area of Ephesus (refer to the letters to the seven churches in Rev. 2–3). He was well-known to his readers.

The letter is addressed "to the chosen lady and her children" (2 John 1). Though some commentators believe this to be a personal letter written to a specific woman and her children, the nature of the letter favors the interpretation that the chosen lady refers to one of the churches in John's charge, and her children were members of that church. The "children of your chosen sister" in verse 13 would then refer to the members of a sister church. No reason is given for such a designation, but it is possible that the threat of persecution (or having a letter to the entire church confiscated by someone such as Diotrephes in 3 John 9–10) prompted John to disguise his recipients.

As in John's first letter, 2 John has as its background the growing threat of false teachers and their possible infiltration into the church. In light of the threat of heresy, it is understandable that John focused so heavily on truth in the first few verses of this letter. It is the truth, after all, that binds believers together. It is the common ground that is the basis of our fellowship with one another (see 1 John 1:7). Truth refers to a set of doctrinal beliefs (who Jesus is, what He taught, and what He did) as well as a moral lifestyle that results from a saving relationship with Christ. So, John could say that "all who know the truth" loved the members of this church "in the truth" (2 John 1) and "because of the truth" (v. 2). And he commended those who were "walking in truth" (v. 4).

Blessings of Living in Truth (2 John 1–3)

Grace, mercy and peace . . . will be with us in truth and love (v. 3). These three blessings—**grace, mercy and peace**—flow from the Father and the Son as we walk in truth and love. As we seek to be faithful and obedient, God pours out His blessings on us. Or the verse may mean that the **grace, mercy and peace** that come from the Father and Son (the result of salvation) will be expressed through **truth and love**.

WORDS FROM WESLEY
2 John 3

Grace—takes away guilt; *Mercy*, misery; *Peace* implies the abiding in grace and mercy. It includes the testimony of God's Spirit, both that we are His children, and that all our ways are acceptable to Him. This is the very foretaste of heaven itself, where it is perfected, *in truth and love*—Or, faith and love, as St. Paul speaks. Faith and truth are here synonymous terms. (ENNT)

Commands for Living in Truth (2 John 4–6)

John gave his readers three commands: They are to walk **in the truth** (v. 4), **walk in obedience**, and **walk in love** (v. 6). And these three are inseparable. John had already linked truth to love (v. 1, "whom I love in the truth," and v. 3, "in truth and love"). He wanted his readers to understand the nature of the Christian walk.

Walk in the Truth. In verse 4, John expressed joy in finding **some of your children walking in the truth, just as the Father commanded us.** The statement is troubling if it indicates that only a small percentage of the church was walking according to the Father's commands. But the word **some** is not in the original language, the text literally reading, "I have found out of your children, ones walking in truth." One would hope that all of the members would be walking in truth, or at least a great number of them. And that may well have been the case. John found joy in those who remained faithful.

Walking in the truth means both believing and obeying what we know to be true. Ignorance of the truth is often used as an excuse for disobedience, but believers have an obligation to know the Father's commands and then to walk in them. The truth was revealed in Jesus (John 14:6) and in God's Word (17:7). Since the truth "lives in us and will be with us forever" (2 John 2; see

Matt. 5:18), we are without excuse when it comes to walking in the truth. The Spirit of Christ living in us guides us into all truth (John 16:13), and His Word is at our ready disposal.

Walk in Obedience. Walking in the truth is **just as the Father commanded us** (2 John 4), so that the one walking in truth will also **walk in obedience to his commands** (v. 6). The true Christian will always exhibit a lifestyle of ready obedience to the commands of God. There is no greater expression of our love for God than the humble submission of obedience (see also John 14:15, 21, 23–24; 1 John 5:3). **This is love: that we walk in obedience to his commands** (2 John 6).

Walk in Love. John wrote, **I am not writing you a new command but one we have had from the beginning. I ask that we love one another** (v. 5). **His command is that you walk in love** (v. 6). The love among Christians is meant to be a witness to the world of the truth of the gospel. But John wasn't talking about sappy sentimentalism here. He was talking about action. And the recipients of that action include other believers: "Therefore, as we have opportunity, let us do good to all people, especially to those who belong to the family of believers" (Gal. 6:10).

WORDS FROM WESLEY

2 John 5

That which we had from the beginning—Of our Lord's ministry. Indeed it was in some sense from the beginning of the world: *that we may love one another*—More abundantly. (ENNT)

There is a tendency today to divorce love and truth, and to expect Christians to be warm and fuzzy in their relationships with all people. We're expected to acquiesce to the demands of others, to keep quiet about sin, to be "nice" to everyone. But love without truth is not really love at all. Paul exhorted us to speak the truth in love (Eph. 4:15). Walking in love of God means walking in obedience to His commands. Walking in love of others means standing firm in the truth and leading them to that truth.

Warnings for Living in Truth (2 John 7–13)

John warned his readers that there are **many deceivers, who . . . have gone out into the world** (v. 7). They don't necessarily come right out and contradict the truth about who Jesus really is. If they did that, Christians would certainly notice immediately the discrepancy with what they formerly had been taught. No, these deceivers **do not acknowledge Jesus Christ as coming in the flesh** (v. 7). They simply fail to acknowledge what is truth. It is a sin of doctrinal omission. And the omission is serious. The person who fails to proclaim the truth about who Jesus is John called **the antichrist** (v. 7; see 1 John 2:22–23). This is why Christians of every age must carefully discern between truth and error (1 John 4:1–3) and must diligently search the Word of God to ensure what we're being taught is true (Acts 17:11).

Watch out that you do not lose what you have worked for, but that you may be rewarded fully (2 John 8). Some believe this verse refers to our salvation, which surely can be lost if we do not continue to walk with Christ (see John 15:6; Rom. 11:22; 1 Tim. 1:19; Heb. 6:4–6). But that would mean John was saying these Christians had worked for their salvation. What they had worked for was certainly some reward (1 Pet. 1:9). Hence the warning that they might not be **rewarded fully** (2 John 8). But what was that reward? Was it a "well done" from our Master or a rich inheritance from the Father (Matt. 25:21, 23; Eph. 6:8; Col. 3:24; Rev. 22:12)? Or did John have in mind what Paul did in 1 Thessalonians 2:19: "For what is our hope, our joy, or the crown in which we will glory in the presence of our Lord Jesus when he comes? Is it not you?" Quite a number of manuscripts have "do not lose what *we* have worked for" instead of "what *you* have worked for," which may indicate that John had the church (and the converts) he had labored for in mind. The church, he said, must guard against heresy and deceivers so his labor wasn't in vain; so the church would continue to grow and stand firm, ultimately leading to a full and rich reward (compare Gal. 4:11).

WORDS FROM WESLEY

2 John 8

That we lose not the things which we have wrought—Which every apostate does, *but receive a full reward*—Having fully employed all our talents to the glory of Him that gave them. Here again the apostle modestly transfers it to himself. (ENNT)

But John also warned them about their own salvation. He borrowed from the Gnostic terminology of the day when he cautioned against **anyone who runs ahead and does not continue** (remain) **in the teaching of Christ** (2 John 9). The Gnostics, with their superior knowledge, believed they were way ahead of the Christians in the church. They were advanced. They had moved ahead to something better. But John said running ahead will get you nowhere. The Christians were to remain in what they had been taught. John said anyone who doesn't remain in Christ's teachings (as recorded in the Gospels, which were being circulated by this time) **does not have God** (v. 9). Notice how John tied the Father and Son together here. If someone doesn't follow Jesus, he or she doesn't have God either. Conversely, **whoever continues in the teaching has both the Father and the Son** (v. 9). Jesus taught that those who had seen Him had seen the Father and that He and the Father were one (John 14:9;

10:30). And that is precisely what John taught here. So those today who contend you can believe in one without the other are wrong. If you don't believe in Jesus, you don't know God, because God has revealed himself through the Son. The Son is God incarnate.

If anyone comes to you and does not bring this teaching (the teaching concerning who Christ really is—God in the flesh) **do not take him into your house or welcome him** (2 John 10). The admonition here isn't against inviting non-Christians or people deceived by a cult into your home to share the gospel with them; it's about inviting those who are teachers of heresy into your home as a means of sustaining them in their ministry. In John's day, itinerant teachers and preachers were common. They traveled from town to town, depending on the generosity of the locals for food and lodging. The singular noun **house** coupled with the plural verbs in this sentence may indicate that the house here is a reference to the church. John may have been warning the church to make sure those they invested in and welcomed into their assembly to teach really were preaching the truth of the gospel. We have an obligation to protect those under our care and to ensure they are being taught correctly (1 Tim. 4:16). **Anyone who welcomes** teachers of false doctrine and makes it possible for them to continue their work **shares in** their **wicked work** (2 John 11).

WORDS FROM WESLEY

2 John 10

If any come to you—Either as a teacher or a brother, *and bring not this doctrine*—That is, advance any thing contrary to it, *receive him not into our house*—As either a teacher or a brother, *neither bid him God speed*—Give him no encouragement therein. (ENNT)

Though John had much more to say, he preferred not **to use paper and ink** (v. 12), preferring a personal visit where he could talk to them **face to face.** His goal was that their **joy may be complete** (v. 12), that both he and the recipients of this message would have a full joy that comes from a knowledge of the truth, obedience to Christ's teachings, and love for the members of God's family (see Phil. 2:2; John 15:11; 1 John 1:4).

DISCUSSION

The Christian life is not a single step, but a walk. We are on an exciting journey, and need to proceed with truth and love in our hearts.

1. Why do you agree or disagree that "the chosen lady and her children" (2 John 1) refers to a church and its members?

2. Do you think it is appropriate that "grace" precedes "mercy and peace" (2 John 3)? Explain your answer.

3. Would you agree that the truth is essential to successful Christian living? Why or why not? See John 17:17.

4. How does John's many references to the truth in 2 John 1–4 build your admiration for the truth?

5. How does the word *walk* shape your concept of the Christian life as a journey, not an occasional step?

6. According to verses 7–8, what dangers confront us on our spiritual journey?

7. What dangers to the Christian life do you think are most prevalent today?

8. How can we overcome every threat we encounter on our spiritual journeys?

PRAYER

Father, help us walk in love, speak the truth with love, and guard our brothers and sisters from those who would lead them astray.

IMITATE WHAT IS GOOD

3 John 1–14

Imitate good not evil.

M ost individuals want to be like someone they admire, whether that person is a highly successful musician, athlete, artist, entrepreneur, scientist, author, teacher, or politician. Of course, it may be impossible to perfectly imitate a famous role model in the secular world, but it is possible to imitate a worthy role model in the church. After all, the Holy Spirit enables us to do so. He wants to develop in us the same graces we see in the life of a godly role model.

This study identifies the kind of role model we should imitate, and it inspires us to become like that person—"well spoken of by everyone" (3 John 12).

COMMENTARY

John's letters offer a valuable glimpse of the state of the church in the latter part of the first century. False teachers announced a message that denied the incarnation of Christ and downplayed the wickedness of sin, distorting the truth of the gospel. John expected true Christians to discern what was true and to take no measures that would contribute to the continuance of such false teaching (2 John 10–11).

John's third letter offers instructions concerning hospitality toward genuine missionaries, who traveled from church to church with the message of the gospel and were worthy of the church's support. Most inns served as brothels, so Jews were dependent on other Jews for overnight lodging, often carrying with them letters of recommendation (attesting to the fact that they were indeed good Jews and worthy of hospitality). The Christians appear to have continued this practice.

Here, in just fourteen verses, John introduced us to three people in the early church: one who was a shining example of what John expected of all Christians, one with a bad attitude who was not to be imitated, and yet another outstanding Christian (probably a traveling missionary) worthy of the church's support.

A Commendation of Gaius (3 John 1–8)

This letter is written **to** John's **dear friend Gaius** (v. 1), yet we don't know any more of this Gaius than what we learn of him in these few verses. Gaius was one of the most common names in the Roman Empire, so this Gaius is not necessarily equated with the others mentioned in Acts, Romans, and 1 Corinthians (but note Rom. 16:23, where Paul commended the hospitality of a man named Gaius in Corinth). John addressed Gaius as his **dear friend** (literally, beloved) in 3 John 1, 2, 5, and 11. Because John referred to Gaius as one **whom I love in the truth** (v. 1) and referred to his joy at hearing **my children are walking in the truth** (v. 4, compare 2 John 4), some have conjectured that Gaius was one of John's converts (see similar designations in Gal. 4:19; 1 Cor. 4:14–15; Phil. 2:22; 1 Tim. 1:2; 1 Thess. 2:11). But it is equally possible that John saw all those under his spiritual care as his children (see 1 John 2:1, 12–13, 18, 28; 3:7, 18; 4:4; 5:21; 2 John 1, 4).

Gaius may have been a leader in the church, since traveling missionaries stayed with him (3 John 5) and John felt comfortable sharing with him the problem with Diotrephes (vv. 9–10). John's opening greeting, **I pray that you may enjoy good health and that all may go well with you** (v. 2), was a sincere wish for success and prosperity, not simply a customary greeting.

Notice, though, the rest of John's sentence: **even as your soul is getting along well** (v. 2). John knew Gaius enough (or had heard sufficient reports, see vv. 3, 6) to be assured that his spiritual life was also prospering.

John's commendation of Gaius is twofold. First, he was commended for his **faithfulness to the truth** (v. 3). Some of his fellow Christians had reported to John how Gaius had continued to **walk in the truth** (v. 3; see 2 John 4). That others bore witness to Gaius's faithfulness is evidence that John was talking about more than just his personally held beliefs. Perhaps Gaius had had opportunity to refute false teachers or to teach correct doctrine to those in his care. He didn't merely keep the truth to himself. Others knew what he believed, and it was obvious to all that Gaius was committed to the truth of the gospel. He believed it and lived it out in his daily walk. This brought John great joy. In fact, John had **no greater joy than to hear that** his **children** were **walking in the truth** (3 John 4).

WORDS FROM WESLEY

3 John 4

I have no greater joy than this—Such is the spirit of every true Christian pastor: *to hear that my children walk in the truth*—Gaius probably was converted by St. Paul. Therefore when St. John speaks of him, with other believers, as his children, it may be considered as the tender style of paternal love, whoever were the instruments of their conversion. And his using this appellation, when writing under the character of the elder, has its peculiar beauty. (ENNT)

John's second commendation of Gaius was for his love: **They have told the church about your love** (v. 6). Gaius was faithful to the truth (v. 3), and he was also **faithful in what** he was **doing**

for the brothers (v. 5). Those who had been recipients of his hospitality had reported the kindness to John. Gaius had provided for these fellow Christians **even though they** were **strangers** (v. 5). Hebrews 13:1–2 reminds us, "Keep on loving each other as brothers. Do not forget to entertain strangers, for by so doing some people have entertained angels without knowing it." Hospitality is a natural overflow of love for people and a desire to please God, but it also results in blessings to us.

John encouraged Gaius to continue in this act of love and also to **send them on their way in a manner worthy of God** (3 John 6). The request is to give these brothers and sisters provision for the journey, treating them as God's representatives. Jesus had taught His disciples that a worker was worth his keep (Matt. 10:10), and Paul had taught that those who preach and teach should receive double honor and respect (1 Tim. 5:17; 1 Thess. 5:12–13) as well as financial support: "Those who preach the gospel should receive their living from the gospel" (see 1 Cor. 9:7–14). These brothers were traveling **for the sake of the Name** (3 John 7), not for their own pleasure or because of greed. And they had no other means of support, choosing not to receive **help from the pagans** (v. 7). It was therefore the obligation (**ought** in v. 8) to **show hospitality to such men** (not to all people, but to those who followed this example). By so doing they became co-laborers, working **together for the truth** (v. 8). In 2 John 11, the apostle warned that anyone offering hospitality to a false teacher "shares in his wicked work," and here he said that those who do offer hospitality to true brothers are workers together for the truth. We should always be careful who we support! Our contributions to the ministry of others is a collaboration in their work, whether for truth or for evil.

A Condemnation of Diotrephes (3 John 9–11)

John's description of Diotrephes in verses 9–11 stands in sharp contrast to his description of Gaius. Apparently, John had written a letter to the entire church (either to the same church Gaius attended, or possibly to a neighboring church with which Gaius was familiar and where Diotrephes held a position of leadership) concerning this matter of hospitality. Since neither 1 John nor 2 John seem likely to be this letter, it is supposed that it was lost through the years, though it is also quite likely that Diotrephes intercepted the letter and confiscated it, not allowing it to even be read to the church. That would certainly fit with his personality described here.

WORDS FROM WESLEY

3 John 9

I wrote to the church—Probably that to which they came: *but Diotrephes*—Perhaps the pastor of it: *who loveth to have the preeminence among them*—To govern all things according to his own will: *receiveth us not*—Neither them nor me. So did the mystery of iniquity already work! (ENNT)

For some unknown reason, Diotrephes struggled with John's authority. Others apparently were reporting to John, and his position as "elder" (3 John 1) may indicate that he exercised oversight of this church, which Diotrephes resented. Instead of submitting to John's authority, he would **have nothing to do with** them (v. 9), **gossiping maliciously about** them (v. 10). People like **Diotrephes, who loves to be first** (v. 9), often attempt to maintain their position of authority by tearing down the reputation of others. Apparently, that's what he was doing with John. He didn't want the competition. Diotrephes didn't stop with bringing false and meaningless charges against the apostle; he refused **to welcome the brothers. He also** stopped **those who** wanted **to do so and** put **them out of the church** (v. 10). Threatened by the popularity (or perhaps the truthfulness) of these itinerant preachers, Diotrephes refused to allow them access to the church and actually reproved others for not following his example.

John urged Gaius, **do not imitate what is evil but what is good** (v. 11). Some commentators argue that John was in no way implying that Diotrephes was not a Christian, just that some of his behavior should not be used as a model for conduct. But nothing could be further from the truth. John continued: **Anyone who does what is evil has not seen God** (v. 11). And how could Diotrephes's actions be seen as anything but evil? The word for **does what is evil** means to do wrong, to harm or injure. Diotrephes was obviously doing wrong to the brothers and was harming John's reputation as well as the health of the entire church. He had a serious sin problem. His actions proved he had not seen God.

John was prepared to step in to help with this problem: **So if I come, I will call attention to what he is doing** (v. 10). Such behavior must be brought into the open, addressed directly, and corrected. But John said **if I come**, not "when I come," which may signal that he was trusting Gaius to intervene in this situation and would only step in if it became necessary.

WORDS FROM WESLEY

3 John 11

*Follow not that which is evil—*In Diotrephes, *but that which is good—*in Demetrius. *He hath not seen God—*Is a stranger to him. (ENNT)

A Recommendation of Demetrius (3 John 12–14)

John told Gaius to imitate what is good, and that "anyone who does what is good is from God" (v. 11). And then he held up Demetrius as an example of one who does what is good. This is not the Demetrius of Acts 19:24 (an enemy of the gospel), nor is there any evidence that this is the Demetrius (or Demas) mentioned in Colossians 4:14; Philemon 24; or 2 Timothy 4:10. Instead, it is wise to take this Demetrius as an otherwise unknown Christian missionary teacher to whom John wanted Gaius to show hospitality in the future. John may in fact have been sending this letter by way of Demetrius as a confirmation that he was worthy of being supported by the church as he shared the gospel with them. John himself vouched for Demetrius's character: **We also speak well of him, and you know that our testimony is true** (3 John 12; see also John 21:24; despite the allegations that may have been made by Diotrephes). But he also offered other evidence: **Demetrius is well spoken of by everyone** (3 John 12). He had a good reputation among all who knew him—not just because he was well liked or popular, but because even **the truth itself** spoke well of him (his genuineness was self-evident; his lifestyle confirmed his faithfulness to the truth). Demetrius was exactly the type of person who should be imitated and honored by the church.

John's closing words in verses 13 and 14 are similar to his ending comments in 2 John 12, though in 2 John he mentioned "paper and ink" versus **pen and ink** (3 John 13) here, and he added that he hoped **to see** Gaius **soon** (v. 14). He was planning to speak to Gaius **face to face.**

John ended with **Peace to you** (v. 14). Perhaps in light of the fact that Diotrephes had caused so much strife John offered a blessing of peace for his friend, knowing that God is more than able to grant it in the church. The final sentences—**The friends here send their greetings. Greet the friends there by name**

(v. 14)—is unique. Perhaps John used the term **friends** (from the Greek *philos*, meaning "dear" or "beloved") instead of the usual *brothers* to remind Gaius of the love he shared with those in other parts of the world and also of John's love for the other members of the church where Gaius worked. John asked Gaius to greet his friends **by name**, a gesture of both intimacy and importance (see John 10:3). Friendship was to be highly valued. John also may have had in mind here Jesus' words recorded in John 15:13–14: "Greater love has no one than this, that he lay down his life for his friends. You are my friends if you do what I command."

WORDS FROM WESLEY

3 John 14

Salute the friends by name—That is, in the same manner as if I had named them one by one. The word *friend* does not often occur in the New Testament, being swallowed up in the more endearing one of *brother*. (ENNT)

DISCUSSION

The early church wasn't perfect, because people aren't perfect. However, when fellow Christians set a good example, we should imitate them.

1. What kind of church member blesses your life? What kind of church member troubles you?

2. How should a church handle a gossiping, egotistical, dictatorial church member?

3. Why do you agree or disagree that Christian hospitality is decreasing?

4. What suggestions would you give a church that wants to experience greater hospitality?

5. What aspect of Christian fellowship gives you great joy? Why?

6. Read 3 John 2–5. How does Gaius's example inspire you?

7. Why should a church support missions? How might the support extend beyond financial support?

8. What characteristics of John shine brightly in 3 John?

9. Why do you think Demetrius was "well spoken of by everyone" (3 John 12)?

10. Would it be a good thing to be well spoken of by everyone in your church? Why or why not?

PRAYER

Father, provide us with strong, godly role models who encourage us to be like You. And help us grow into these role models ourselves.

WORDS FROM WESLEY WORKS CITED

ENNT: *Explanatory Notes upon the New Testament,* by John Wesley, M.A. Fourth American Edition. New York: J. Soule and T. Mason, for the Methodist Episcopal Church in the United States, 1818.

PW: *The Poetical Works of John and Charles Wesley.* Edited by D. D. G. Osborn. 13 vols. London: Wesleyan-Methodist Conference Office, 1868.

WJW: *The Works of John Wesley.* Third Edition, Complete and Unabridged. 14 vols. London: Wesleyan Methodist Book Room, 1872.

OTHER BOOKS IN THE
WESLEY BIBLE STUDIES SERIES

Genesis (available February 2015)
Exodus (available April 2015)
Leviticus through Deuteronomy (available June 2015)
Joshua through Ruth (available June 2015)
1 Samuel through 2 Chronicles (available February 2015)
Ezra through Esther (available April 2015)
Job through Song of Songs (available February 2015)
Isaiah (available April 2015)
Jeremiah through Daniel (available February 2015)
Hosea through Malachi (available June 2015)
Matthew
Mark
Luke (available September 2014)
John
Acts (available September 2014)
Romans
1–2 Corinthians (available September 2014)
Galatians through Colossians and Philemon
1–2 Thessalonians (available September 2014)
1 Timothy through Titus
Hebrews
James
1–2 Peter and Jude
1–3 John
Revelation

Now Available in the
Wesley Bible Studies Series

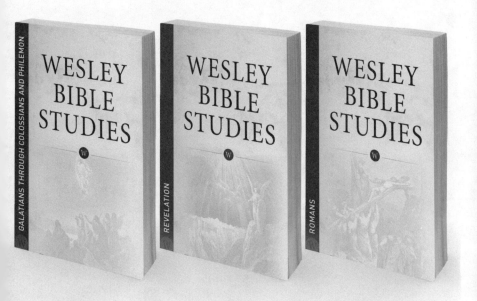

Each book in the Wesley Bible Studies series provides a thoughtful and powerful survey of key Scriptures in one or more biblical books. They combine accessible commentary from contemporary teachers, with relevantly highlighted direct quotes from the complete writings and life experiences of John Wesley, along with the poetry and hymns of his brother Charles. For each study, creative and engaging questions foster deeper fellowship and growth.

Galatians through Colossians and Philemon
978-0-89827-864-4
978-0-89827-865-1 (e-book)

Romans
978-0-89827-854-5
978-0-89827-855-2 (e-book)

Revelation
978-0-89827-878-1
978-0-89827-879-8 (e-book)

wphonline.com
1.800.493.7539